Fort Scott National Historic Site Visitor Study

Summer 2011

Natural Resource Report NPS/NRSS/EQD/NRR—2012/540

Marc F. Manni, Yen Le, Steven J. Hollenhorst

Visitor Services Project
Park Studies Unit
University of Idaho
Moscow, ID 83844-1139

June 2012

U.S. Department of the Interior
National Park Service
Natural Resource Stewardship and Science
Fort Collins, Colorado

The National Park Service, Natural Resource Stewardship and Science office in Fort Collins, Colorado publishes a range of reports that address natural resource topics of interest and applicability to a broad audience in the National Park Service and others in natural resource management, including scientists, conservation and environmental constituencies, and the public.

The Natural Resource Report Series is used to disseminate high-priority, current natural resource management information with managerial application. The series targets a general, diverse audience, and may contain NPS policy considerations or address sensitive issues of management applicability.

All manuscripts in the series receive the appropriate level of peer review to ensure that the information is scientifically credible, technically accurate, appropriately written for the intended audience, and designed and published in a professional manner.

Data in this report were collected and analyzed using methods based on established, peer-reviewed protocols and were analyzed and interpreted within the guidelines of the protocols.

Views, statements, findings, conclusions, recommendations, and data in this report do not necessarily reflect views and policies of the National Park Service, U.S. Department of the Interior. Mention of trade names or commercial products does not constitute endorsement or recommendation for use by the U.S. Government.

This report is available from the Social Science Division (http://www.nature.nps.gov/socialscience/index.cfm) and the Natural Resource Publications Management website (http://www.nature.nps.gov/publications/nrpm/).

This report and other reports by the Visitor Services Project (VSP) are available from the VSP website (http://www.psu.uidaho.edu/c5/vsp/vsp-reports/) or by contacting the VSP office at (208) 885-7863.

Please cite this publication as:

Manni, M. F., Y. Le, & S. J. Hollenhorst. 2012. Fort Scott National Historic Site visitor study: Summer 2011. Natural Resource Report NPS/NRSS/EQD/NRR—2012/540. National Park Service, Fort Collins, Colorado.

NPS 471/115207, June 2012

Contents

Page

Contents (continued)

Executive Summary

This visitor study report profiles a systematic, random sample of Fort Scott National Historic Site (NHS) visitors during July 15 – August 23, 2011. A total of 341 questionnaires were distributed to visitor groups. Of those, 248 questionnaires were returned, resulting in a 72.7% response rate.

Group size and type	Forty-six percent of visitor groups consisted of two people, while 30% consisted of four or more people. Seventy-four percent of visitor groups consisted of family groups.
State or country of residence	United States visitors were from 33 states and comprised 99% of total visitation during the survey period, with 34% from Kansas. International visitors were too few in number to provide reliable information.
Frequency of visits	Seventy-five percent of visitors were visiting the park for the first time, while 17% had visited two or three times.
Age, gender, ethnicity, and race	Forty percent of visitors were ages 55 to 70 years old, 21% were 15 years or younger, 18% were 36 to 50 years old, and 9% were 71 years or older. Fifty-one percent of respondents were male; 49% were female. Two percent of visitors were Hispanic or Latino. Most visitors (95%) were White.
Educational level and income level	Thirty percent of respondents had completed a graduate degree and 28% had a bachelor's degree. Twenty-seven percent of respondents reported a household income of $50,000-$74,000.
Physical conditions	Nine percent of visitor groups had members with physical conditions affecting their ability to access or participate in activities or services.
Awareness of park management	Fifty-nine percent of visitor groups were aware that Fort Scott NHS is a unit of the National Park System.
Information sources	Most visitor groups (77%) obtained information about the park prior to their visit through friends/relatives/word of mouth (35%), maps/brochures (35%), and the park website (34%). Most visitor groups (95%) received the information they needed. Sixty-eight percent of visitor groups preferred to use the park website to obtain information for a future visit.
Park as destination	For 41% of visitor groups, the park was not a planned destination, while for 30%, the park was the primary destination.
Primary reason for visiting the area	Three percent of visitor groups were residents of Fort Scott, KS. The most common primary reasons for visiting the park area among non-resident visitor groups were to visit the park (42%) and traveling through – unplanned visit (31%).
Services used in nearby communities	Fifty-four percent of visitor groups obtained support services in nearby communities. The communities most often used included Fort Scott, KS (66%), Pittsburg, KS (19%), and Nevada, MO (16%). Ninety-six percent of visitor groups were able to obtain needed support services in nearby communities.
Overnight stays	Eighteen percent of visitor groups stayed overnight in Fort Scott, KS, of which 60% stayed one night, while 24% stayed two nights. Sixty-seven percent of visitor groups stayed in lodges, hotels, motels, vacation rentals, B&Bs, etc.

Executive Summary (continued)

Length of stay
The average length of stay for visitor groups was 1.6 hours. Two percent of visitor groups visited the park on more than one day.

Local and regional attractions
Sixty-three percent of visitor groups visited local and regional attractions. The most commonly visited attractions were downtown Fort Scott (63%), Fort Scott National Cemetery (26%), and Mine Creek Battlefield (19%).

Activities on this visit
The most common activities of visitor groups were general sightseeing (85%), viewing indoor exhibits and furnished rooms (83%), and viewing outdoor exhibits and buildings (82%).

Talks, programs, and tours
Eight-two percent of visitor groups took the self-guided brochure tour and (8%) took the cell phone tour. Twenty-six percent of visitor groups attended a ranger or volunteer-led talk, program, or tour on this visit. Of those, 43% took a guided tour and 39% attended a talk. Fifty-six percent of visitor groups preferred a program length of 1/2 to 1 hour.

Information services and facilities
The information services and facilities most commonly used by visitor groups were the indoor exhibits (86%), park brochure/map (79%), restrooms (78%), and visitor center – Post Hospital (75%).

Quality of interaction with park staff
Most visitor groups (94%) had personal interactions with park staff on this visit. The combined proportions of "very good" and "good" ratings of the quality of interaction with park staff were courteousness (98%), quality of information provided (98%), and helpfulness (97%).

Expenditures
The average visitor group expenditure (inside the park and in Fort Scott, KS) was $75. The median group expenditure (50% of groups spent more and 50% of groups spent less) was $25, and the average total expenditure per person (per capita) was $35.

Future visits to the park
Sixty-seven percent of visitor groups indicated they would likely visit the park in the future, while 21% were not sure if they would. Ninety-five percent of visitor groups were interested in learning about the park's cultural and natural history/features on a future visit through a self-guided tour with brochure (67%), indoor exhibits (61%), and outdoor exhibits (60%).

Overall quality
Most visitor groups (97%) rated the overall quality of facilities, services, and recreational opportunities at Fort Scott NHS as "very good" or "good". No visitor groups rated the quality as "poor," while 1% rated the quality as "very poor."

For more information about the Visitor Services Project, please contact the Park Studies Unit at the University of Idaho at (208) 885-7863 or the following website http://www.psu.uidaho.edu.

Acknowledgements

We thank Marc Manni for compiling the report, Nancy Holmes for overseeing the fieldwork, the staff and volunteers of Fort Scott NHS for assisting with the survey, and David Vollmer and Matthew Strawn for data processing.

About the Authors

Marc Manni is the Research Team Supervisor for the Visitor Services Project. Yen Le, Ph.D., is Assistant Director of the Visitor Services Project at the University of Idaho. Steven Hollenhorst, Ph.D., is the Director of the Park Studies Unit, Department of Conservation Social Sciences, University of Idaho.

Introduction

This report describes the results of a visitor study at Fort Scott National Historic Site (NHS) in Fort Scott, KS conducted July 15 – August 23, 2011 by the National Park Service (NPS) Visitor Services Project (VSP), part of the Park Studies Unit (PSU) at the University of Idaho.

As described in the National Park Service website for Fort Scott NHS, "The story of Fort Scott is the story of America growing up. When the fort was established in 1842, the nation was still young and confined largely to the area east of the Mississippi River. Yet within a few years, Fort Scott's soldiers became involved in events that would lead to tremendous spurts of growth and expansion. As the nation developed, tensions over slavery led to the conflict and turmoil of "Bleeding Kansas" and the Civil War. Fort Scott takes you through these years of crisis and beyond to the time when the United States emerged as a united, transcontinental nation." (www.nps.gov/fosc, retrieved April 2012).

Organization of the Report

This report is organized into three sections.

Section 1: **Methods**
This section discusses the procedures, limitations, and special conditions that may affect the study results.

Section 2: **Results**
This section provides a summary for each question in the questionnaire and includes visitor comments to open-ended questions. The presentation of the results of this study does not follow the order of questions in the questionnaire.

Section 3: **Appendices**
Appendix 1. *The Questionnaire.* A copy of the questionnaire distributed to visitor groups.

Appendix 2. *Additional Analysis.* A list of sample questions for cross-references and cross comparisons. Comparisons can be analyzed within a park or between parks. Results of additional analyses are not included in this report.

Appendix 3. *Decision Rules for Checking Non-response Bias.* An explanation of how the non-response bias was determined.

Presentation of the Results

Results are represented in the form of graphs (see example below), scatter plots, pie charts, tables, and text.

SAMPLE

1. The figure title describes the graph's information.

2. Listed above the graph, the "N" shows the number of individuals or visitor groups responding to the question. If "N" is less than 30, "**CAUTION!**" is shown on the graph to indicate the results may be unreliable.

 * appears when the total percentages do not equal 100 due to rounding.

** appears when total percentages do not equal 100 because visitors could select more than one answer choice.

3. Vertical information describes the response categories.

4. Horizontal information shows the number or proportion of responses in each category.

5. In most graphs, percentages provide additional information.

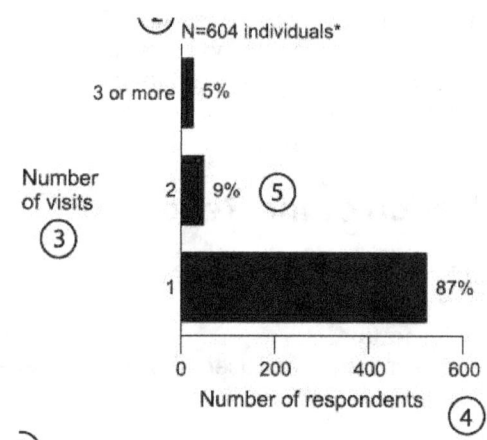

Methods

Survey Design and Procedures

Sample size and sampling plan

All VSP questionnaires follow design principles outlined in Don A. Dillman's book *Mail and Internet Surveys: The Tailored Design Method* (2007). Using this method, the sample size was calculated based on the park's visitation statistics of previous years.

Brief interviews were conducted with a systematic, random sample of visitor groups that arrived at the fort during July 15 – August 23, 2011, reaching virtually every group that entered the site. Visitors were surveyed between the hours of 8 a.m. and 5 p.m. During this survey, 352 visitor groups were contacted and 341 of these groups (96.9%) accepted questionnaires. (The average acceptance rate for 250 VSP visitor studies conducted from 1988 through 2011 is 91.5%.) Questionnaires were completed and returned by 248 respondents, resulting in a 72.7% response rate for this study. (The average response rate for the 250 VSP visitor studies is 72.3%.)

Questionnaire design

The Fort Scott NHS questionnaire was developed through conference calls between the park and the VSP staff to design and prioritize questions. Some of the questions were comparable with VSP studies conducted at other parks while others were customized for Fort Scott NHS. Many questions ask respondents to choose answers from a list of responses, often with an open-ended option, while others are completely open-ended.

No pilot study was conducted to test the Fort Scott NHS questionnaire. However, all questions followed Office Management and Budget (OMB) guidelines and/or were used in previous surveys; thus, the clarity and consistency of the survey instrument have been tested and supported.

Survey procedure

Visitor groups were greeted, briefly introduced to the purpose of the study, and asked to participate. If visitors agreed, they were asked which member (at least 16 years old) had the next birthday. The individual with the next birthday was selected to complete the questionnaire for the group. An interview, lasting approximately two minutes, was conducted with that person to determine group size, group type, the age of the member completing the questionnaire, and how this visit to the park fit into their group's travel plans. These individuals were asked their names, addresses, and telephone numbers or email addresses in order to mail them a reminder/thank-you postcard and follow-ups. Participants were asked to complete the survey after their visit, and return it using the Business Reply Mail envelope provided.

Two weeks following the survey, a reminder/thank-you postcard was mailed to all participants who provided a valid mailing address (see Table 1). Replacement questionnaires were mailed to participants who had not returned their questionnaires four weeks after the survey. Seven weeks after the survey, a second round of replacement questionnaires was mailed to participants who had not returned their questionnaires.

Table 1. Follow-up mailing distribution

Round 1 Mailing	Date	U.S.	International	Total
Postcards	August 12, 2011	166	5	171
1st replacement	August 26, 2011	76	3	79
2nd replacement	September 16, 2011	66	0	66

Round 2 Mailing	Date	U.S.	International	Total
Postcards	August 26, 2011	95	1	96
1st replacement	September 9, 2011	43	1	44
2nd replacement	September 29, 2011	33	0	33

Round 3 Mailing	Date	U.S.	International	Total
Postcards	September 8, 2011	70	2	72
1st replacement	September 23, 2011	26	1	27
2nd replacement	October 12, 2011	23	0	23

Data analysis

Returned questionnaires were coded and the responses were processed using custom and standard statistical software applications—Statistical Analysis Software® (SAS), and a custom designed FileMaker Pro® application. Descriptive statistics and cross-tabulations were calculated for the coded data; responses to open-ended questions were categorized and summarized. Double-key data entry validation was performed on numeric and text entry variables and the remaining checkbox (bubble) variables were read by optical mark recognition (OMR) software.

Limitations

As with all surveys, this study has limitations that should be considered when interpreting the results.

1. This was a self-administered survey. Respondents completed the questionnaire after their visit, which may have resulted in poor recall. Thus, it is not possible to know whether visitor responses reflected actual behavior.

2. The data reflect visitor use patterns at the selected sites during the study period of July 15 – August 23, 2011. The results present a 'snapshot in time' and do not necessarily apply to visitors during other times of the year.

3. Caution is advised when interpreting any data with a sample size of less than 30, as the results may be unreliable. When the sample size is less than 30, the word "**CAUTION!**" is included in the graph, figure, table, or text.

4. Occasionally, there may be inconsistencies in the results. Inconsistencies arise from missing data or incorrect answers (due to misunderstood directions, carelessness, or poor recall of information). Therefore, refer to both the percentage and N (number of individuals or visitor groups) when interpreting the results.

Special conditions

The weather during the survey period ranged from mild and rainy to hot, humid, and sunny, with daily high temperatures ranging from 81°F to 112°F.

No special events were held that could have affected the type and amount of visitation to the park.

Checking non-response bias

Five variables were used to check non-response bias: participant age, group size, group type, park as destination, and participant proximity from home to the park. All variables were found to have insignificant differences between respondents and non-respondents except for average age (see Tables 2 - 5). There is a potential bias toward respondents at higher age ranges (especially 50 and older). See Appendix 3 for more details of the non-response bias checking procedures.

Table 2. Comparison of respondents and non-respondents by average age and group size

Variable	Respondents	Non-respondents	p-value (t-test)
Age (years)	55.39 (N=247)	56.34 (N=93)	<0.001
Group size	2.92 (N=246)	2.99 (N=90)	0.757

Table 3. Comparison of respondents and non-respondents by group type

Group type	Respondents	Non-respondents	p-value (chi-square)
Alone	35	7	
Family	183	65	
Friends	15	12	
Family and friends	12	5	
Other	1	1	
			0.129

Table 4. Comparison of respondents and non-respondents by primary destination

Destination	Respondents	Non-respondents	p-value (chi-square)
Park as primary destination	97	33	
Park as one of several destinations	98	30	
Unplanned visit	50	30	
			0.068

Table 5. Comparison of respondents and non-respondents by distance from home to park

Destination	Respondents	Non-respondents	p-value (chi-square)
Within 50 miles	28	12	
51-100 miles	61	32	
101-200 miles	34	15	
201 miles or more	115	29	
International visitors	6	2	
			0.161

Results

Group and Visitor Characteristics

Visitor group size

Question 24b
On this visit, how many people were in your personal group, including yourself?

Results
- 46% of visitor groups consisted of two people (see Figure 1).

- 30% were in groups of four or more.

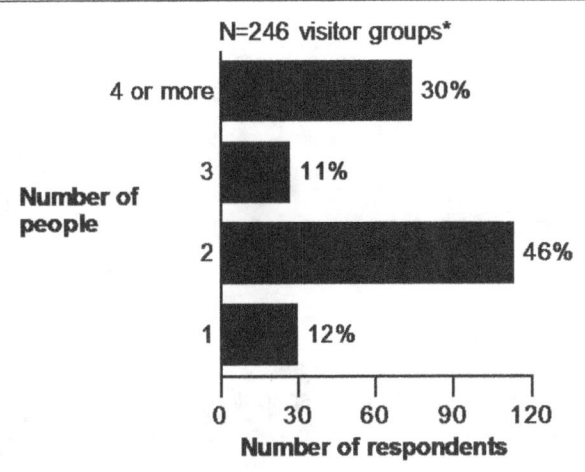

Figure 1. Visitor group size

Visitor group type

Question 24a
On this visit, which type of personal group (not guided tour/school/other organized group) were you with?

Results
- 74% of visitor groups consisted of family members (see Figure 2).

- 14% were alone.

- "Other" group (<1%) was:

    Business

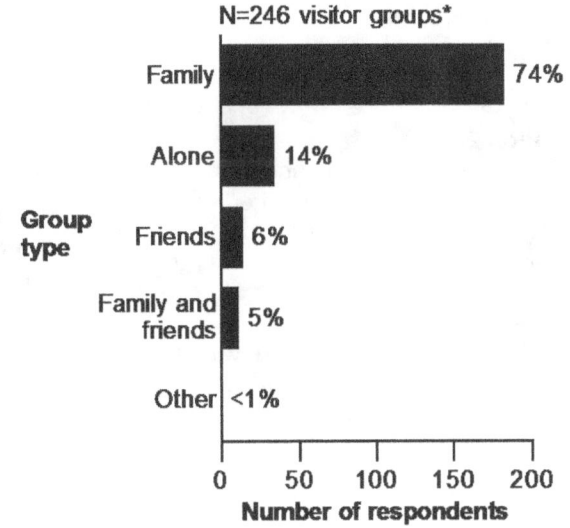

Figure 2. Visitor group type

---

*total percentages do not equal 100 due to rounding
**total percentages do not equal 100 because visitors could select more than one answer

Visitors with organized groups

Question 23a

On this visit, were you and your personal group with a commercial guided tour group?

Results
- <1% of visitor groups were with a commercial guided tour (see Figure 3).

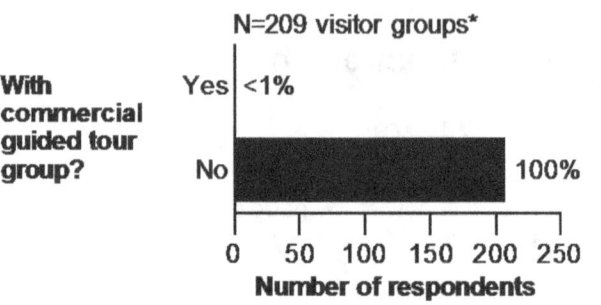

Figure 3. Visitors with a commercial guided tour group

Question 23b

On this visit, were you and your personal group with a school/ educational group?

Results
- <1% of visitor groups were with a school/educational group (see Figure 4).

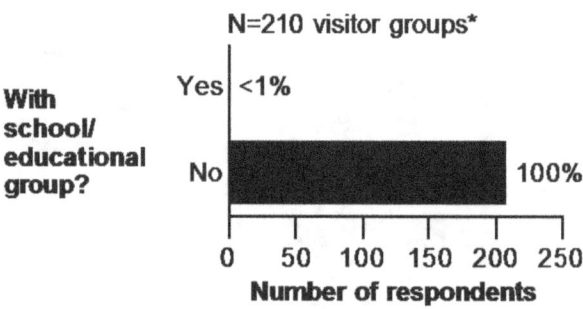

Figure 4. Visitors with a school/educational group

Question 23c

On this visit, were you and your personal group with an "other" organized group (scouts, work, church)?

Results
- 1% of visitor groups were with an "other" organized group (see Figure 5).

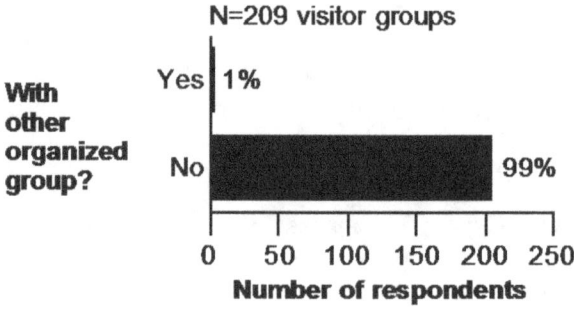

Figure 5. Visitors with an "other" organized group

*total percentages do not equal 100 due to rounding
**total percentages do not equal 100 because visitors could select more than one answer

Question 23d

If you were with one of these organized groups, how many people, including yourself, were in this group?

Results – Interpret results with **CAUTION!**

- Not enough visitor groups responded to this question to provide reliable results (see Figure 6).

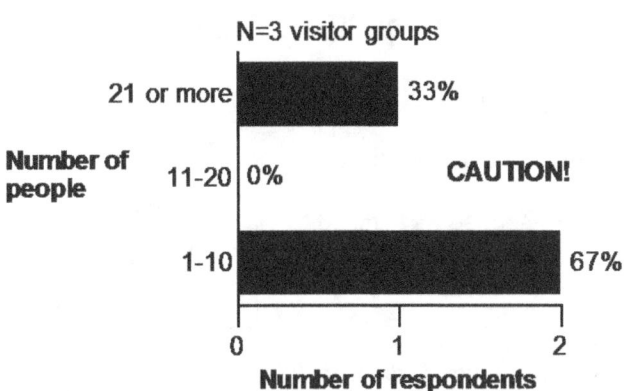

Figure 6. Organized group size

---
*total percentages do not equal 100 due to rounding
**total percentages do not equal 100 because visitors could select more than one answer

United States visitors by state of residence

Question 27b

For your and your personal group on this visit, what is your state of residence?

Note: Response was limited to seven members from each visitor group.

Results

- U.S. visitors were from 33 states and comprised 99% of total visitation to the park during the survey period.

- 34% of U.S. visitors came from Kansas (see Table 6 and Figure 7).

- 18% were from Missouri.

- Smaller proportions came from 31 other states.

Table 6. United States visitors by state of residence

State	Number of visitors	Percent of U.S. visitors N=593 individuals*	Percent of total visitors N=602 individuals
Kansas	202	34	34
Missouri	106	18	18
Texas	51	9	8
Arkansas	24	4	4
California	22	4	4
Illinois	19	3	3
Iowa	15	3	2
Oklahoma	13	2	2
Nebraska	12	2	2
Ohio	11	2	2
Florida	10	2	2
New York	9	2	1
21 other states	99	17	16

N = 593 individuals

%

2% to 3%

less than 2%

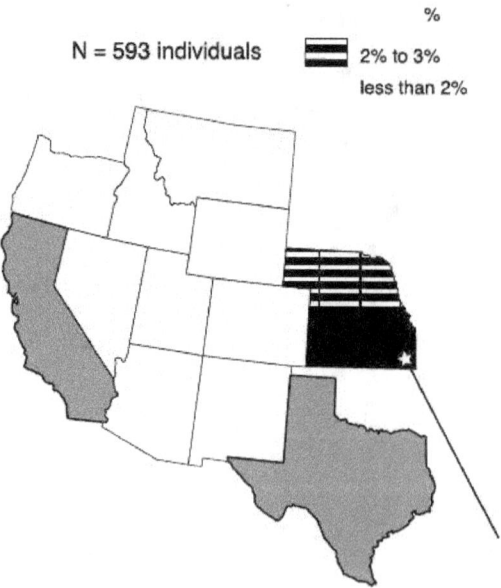

Figure 7. United States visitors by state of residence

*total percentages do not equal 100 due to rounding
**total percentages do not equal 100 because visitors could select more than one answer

Visitors from Kansas and Missouri by county of residence

Note: Response was limited to seven members from each visitor group.

Results
- Visitors from Kansas and Missouri were from 52 counties and comprised 52% of the total U.S. visitation to the park during the survey period.

- 13% came from Johnson, KS (see Table 7).

- 10% came from Shawnee, KS.

- Smaller proportions of visitors came from 50 other counties in Kansas and Missouri.

Table 7. Visitors from Kansas and Missouri by county of residence

County, State	Number of visitors N=308 individuals	Percent
Johnson, KS	41	13
Shawnee, KS	32	10
Bourbon, KS	21	7
Sedgwick, KS	21	7
Jackson, MO	18	6
Jasper, MO	14	5
Douglas, KS	12	4
Crawford, KS	9	3
Cass, MO	8	3
Greene, MO	8	3
Leavenworth, KS	8	3
Laclede, MO	7	2
Linn, KS	6	2
Riley, KS	6	2
St. Charles, MO	6	2
Jefferson, KS	5	2
Miami, KS	5	2
Barton, MO	4	1
Cedar, MO	4	1
Cherokee, KS	4	1
St. Louis, MO	4	1
Vernon, MO	4	1
Barton, KS	3	1
Benton, MO	3	1
Christian, MO	3	1
Coffey, KS	3	1
Hickory, MO	3	1
Lyon, KS	3	1
Neosho, KS	3	1
Polk, MO	3	1
Ray, MO	3	1
Brown, KS	2	1
Camden, MO	2	1
Clay, KS	2	1
Ford, KS	2	1
Henry, MO	2	1
Howell, MO	2	1
Lafayette, MO	2	1
Lawrence, MO	2	1
Morris, KS	2	1
Phillips, KS	2	1

*total percentages do not equal 100 due to rounding
**total percentages do not equal 100 because visitors could select more than one answer

Table 7. Visitors from Kansas and Missouri by county of residence (continued)

County, State	Number of visitors N=308 individuals	Percent
Reno, KS	2	1
Taney, MO	2	1
Thomas, KS	2	1
Allen, KS	1	<1
Butler, MO	1	<1
Franklin, KS	1	<1
Labette, KS	1	<1
St. Louis (city), MO	1	<1
Sumner, KS	1	<1
Wichita, KS	1	<1
Wilson, KS	1	<1

*total percentages do not equal 100 due to rounding
**total percentages do not equal 100 because visitors could select more than one answer

International visitors by country of residence

Question 27b

For your personal group on this visit, what is your country of residence?

Note: Response was limited to seven members from each visitor group.

Results – Interpret with **CAUTION!**

- International visitors were from 4 countries and comprised 1% of total visitation to the park during the survey period.

- 56% of international visitors came from the United Kingdom (see Table 8).

- 22% came from Canada.

Table 8. International visitors by county of residence – **CAUTION!**

Country	Number of visitors	Percent of international visitors N=9 individuals	Percent of total visitors N=602 individuals
United Kingdom	5	56	1
Canada	2	22	<1
Germany	1	11	<1
Mexico	1	11	<1

Number of visits to park

Question 27c

For you and your personal group on this visit, how many times have you visited Fort Scott NHS (including this visit)?

Note: Response was limited to seven members from each visitor group.

Results

- 75% of visitors were visiting the park for the first time (see Figure 8).

- 17% had visited two to three times.

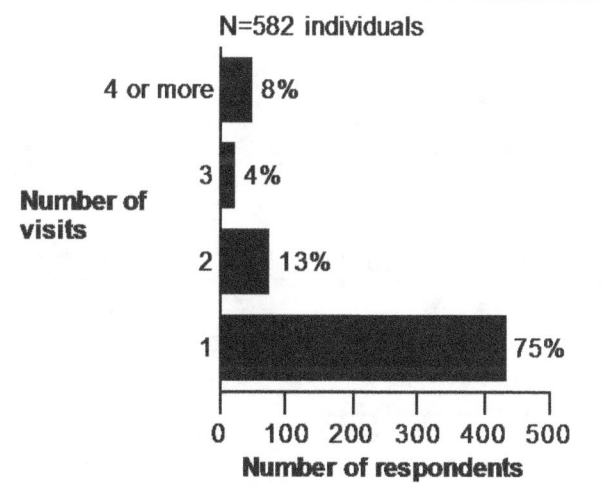

Figure 8. Number of visits to park

*total percentages do not equal 100 due to rounding

**total percentages do not equal 100 because visitors could select more than one answer

Visitor age

Question 27a

For you and your personal group on this visit, what is your current age?

Note: Response was limited to seven members from each visitor group.

Results

- Visitor ages ranged from 1 to 90 years.

- 40% of visitors were 55 to 70 years old (see Figure 9).

- 21% were 15 years or younger.

- 18% were 36 to 50 years old.

- 9% were 71 years or older.

N=653 individuals

Age group (years)	Percent
76 or older	4%
71-75	5%
66-70	8%
61-65	13%
56-60	11%
51-55	8%
46-50	7%
41-45	6%
36-40	5%
31-35	3%
26-30	3%
21-25	2%
16-20	4%
11-15	9%
10 or younger	12%

Figure 9. Visitor age

Respondent gender

Question 26

For you only, what is your gender?

Results

- 51% of respondents were male (see Figure 10).

- 49% were female.

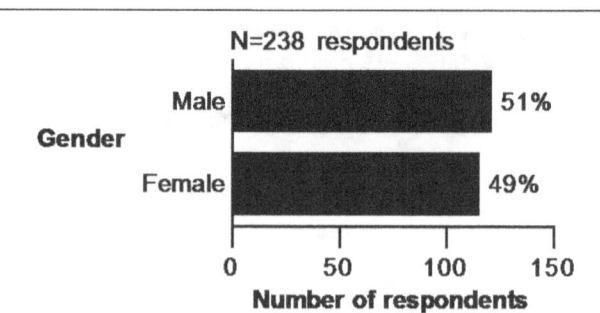

N=238 respondents

Gender	Percent
Male	51%
Female	49%

Figure 10. Respondent gender

---

*total percentages do not equal 100 due to rounding

**total percentages do not equal 100 because visitors could select more than one answer

Visitor ethnicity

Question 28a

Are you or members of your personal group Hispanic or Latino?

Note: Response was limited to seven members from each visitor group.

Results

- 2% of visitors were Hispanic or Latino (see Figure 11).

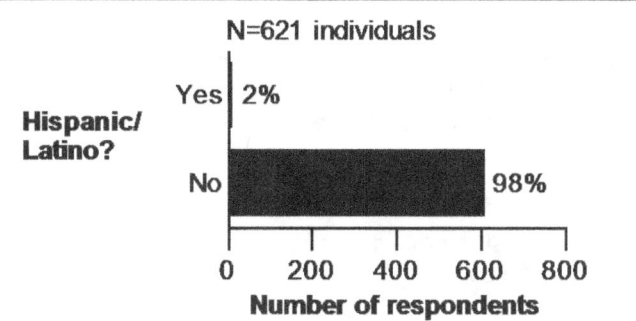

Figure 11. Visitors who were Hispanic or Latino

Visitor race

Question 28b

What is your race? What is the race of each member of your personal group?

Note: Response was limited to seven members from each visitor group.

Results

- 95% of visitors were White (see Figure 12).

- 3% were of more than one race.

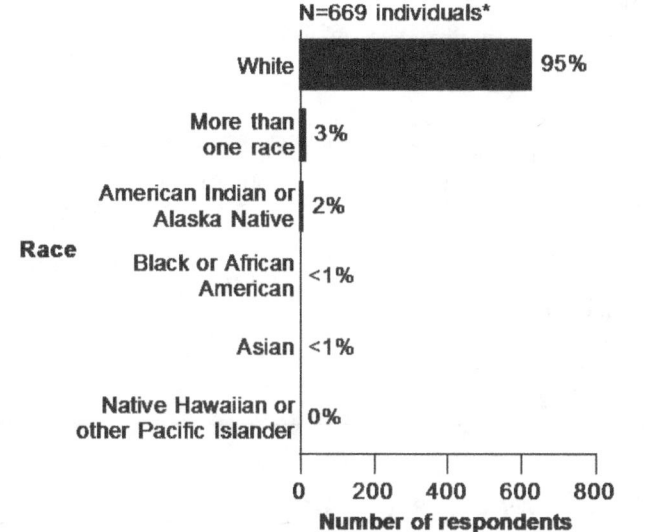

Figure 12. Visitor race

---

*total percentages do not equal 100 due to rounding

**total percentages do not equal 100 because visitors could select more than one answer

Visitors with physical conditions affecting access/participation

Question 29a

Does anyone in your personal group have a physical condition that made it difficult to access or participate in park activities or services?

Results

- 9% of visitor groups had members with physical conditions (see Figure 13).

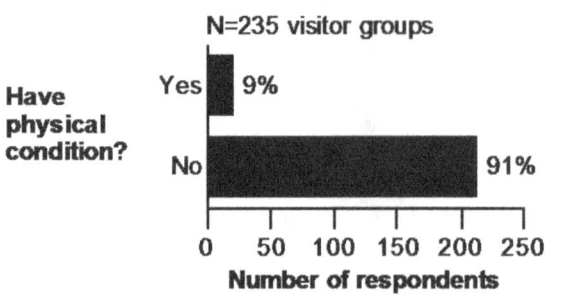

Figure 13. Visitor groups that had members with physical conditions affecting access or participation in park activities or services

Question 29b

If YES, what services or activities were difficult to access/participate in? (Open-ended)

Results – Interpret results with **CAUTION!**

- 19 visitor groups responded to the question, which is insufficient data to provide reliable results (see Table 9).

Table 9. Services/activities that were difficult to access/participate in (N=21 comments; some visitor groups made more than one comment.) – **CAUTION!**

Service/activity	Number of times mentioned
Climbing stairs	16
Walking	3
Arthritis	1
No handrails on sidewalk steps	1

Respondent level of education

Question 25

For you only, what is the highest level of education you have completed?

Results

- 30% of respondents had a graduate degree (see Figure 14).

- 28% had a bachelor's degree.

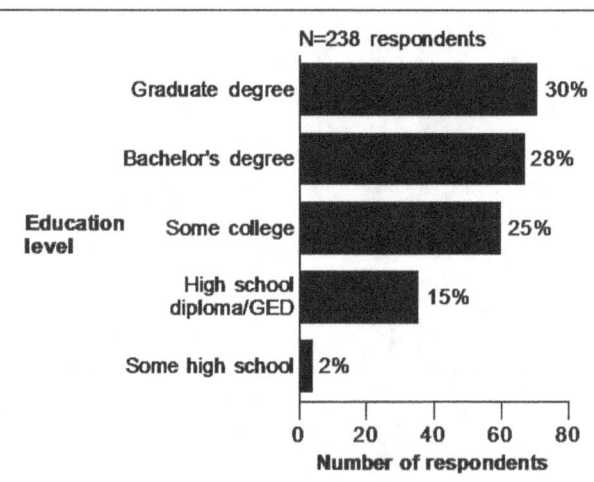

Figure 14. Respondent level of education

---

*total percentages do not equal 100 due to rounding

**total percentages do not equal 100 because visitors could select more than one answer

Respondent household income

Question 22a
Which category best represents your annual household income?

Results
- 27% of respondents reported a household income of $50,000-$74,000 (see Figure 15).

- 15% had an income of $75,000-$99,999.

- 14% had an income of $100,000-$149,999.

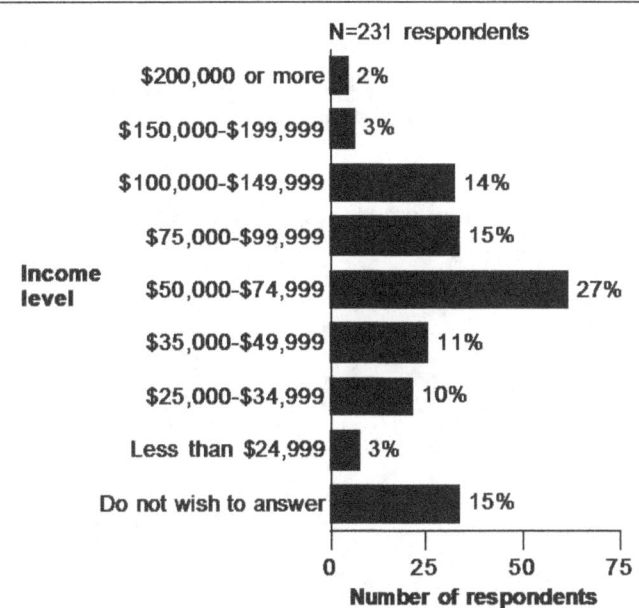

Figure 15. Respondent level of income

Respondent household size

Question 22b
How many people are in your household?

Results
- 56% of respondents had two people in their household (see Figure 16).

- 35% had three or more people.

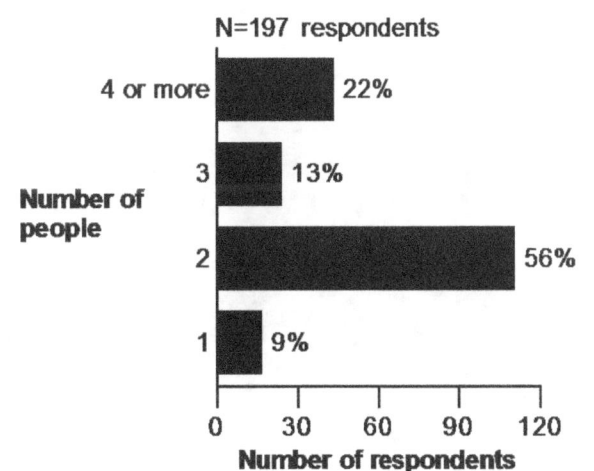

Figure 16. Number of people in household

*total percentages do not equal 100 due to rounding
**total percentages do not equal 100 because visitors could select more than one answer

Awareness of park management

Question 2

Prior to this visit, were you and your personal group aware that Fort Scott NHS is a unit of the National Park System?

Results

- 59% of visitor groups were aware that Fort Scott NHS is a unit of the National Park System (see Figure 17).

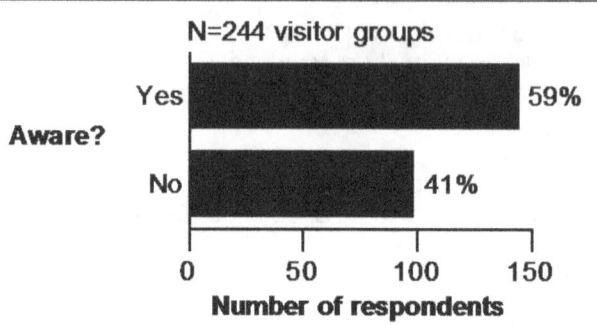

Figure 17. Visitor groups aware that Fort Scott NHS is a unit of the National Park System

---

*total percentages do not equal 100 due to rounding

**total percentages do not equal 100 because visitors could select more than one answer

Trip/Visit Characteristics and Preferences

Information sources prior to visit

Question 1a

Prior to this visit, how did you and your personal group obtain information about Fort Scott NHS?

Results

- 77% of visitor groups obtained information about Fort Scott NHS prior to their visit (see Figure 18).

- As shown in Figure 19, among those visitor groups that obtained information about Fort Scott NHS prior to their visit, the most common sources were:

  35% Friends/relatives/word of mouth
  35% Maps/brochures
  34% Fort Scott NHS website

- "Other" websites (4%) were:

  Fort Scott Chamber of Commerce
  Fort Scott city website
  Google Earth
  k-state.com
  Kansas Civil War sites

- "Other" sources (12%) were:

  Live in area
  Driving by
  General knowledge
  History books
  National Park Passport
  Road signs
  Junior Ranger program
  National Association for
      Interpretation
  NPS passport
  Official guide to national parks
  Road sign
  Visits to other forts
  American Volkssport Association (AVA)

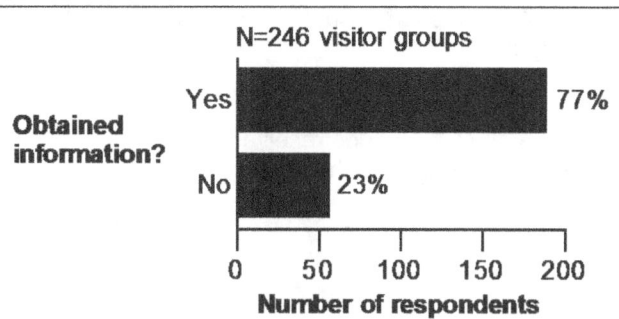

Figure 18. Visitor groups that obtained information prior to visit

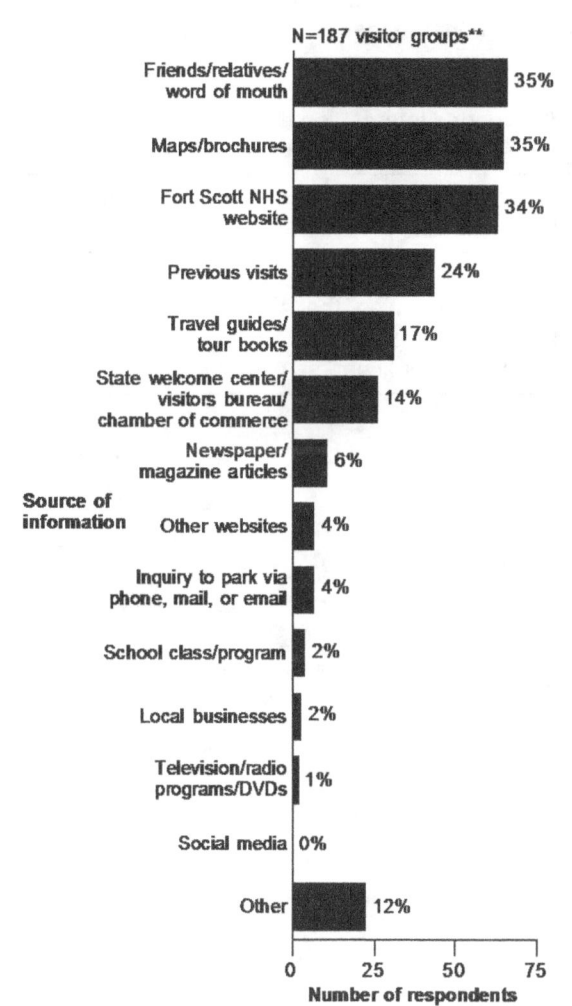

Figure 19. Sources of information used by visitor groups prior to visit

---

*total percentages do not equal 100 due to rounding
**total percentages do not equal 100 because visitors could select more than one answer

Question 1c

From the sources you used prior to this visit, did you and your personal group receive the type of information about the park that you needed?

Results
- 95% of visitor groups received needed information prior to their visit (see Figure 20).

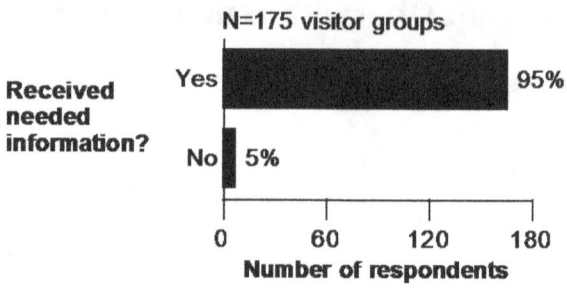

Figure 20. Visitor groups that received needed information prior to their visit

Question 1d

If NO, what type of park information did you and your personal group need that was not available? (Open-ended)

Results – Interpret results with **CAUTION!**
- Three visitor groups listed information they needed but was not available, which is insufficient to provide reliable results (see Table 10).

Table 10. Needed information that was not available (N=3 comments) – **CAUTION!**

Needed information	Number of times mentioned
Map of the site	1
More in-depth information, that's available at the site	1
Passport to the national parks	1

---

*total percentages do not equal 100 due to rounding
**total percentages do not equal 100 because visitors could select more than one answer

Information sources for a future visit

Question 1b

If you were to visit Fort Scott NHS in the future, how would you and your personal group prefer to obtain information about the park?

Results

- As shown in Figure 21, visitor groups' most preferred sources of information for a future visit were:

  68% Park website
  30% Previous visits
  29% Maps/brochures

- "Other" websites (5%) were:

  Cell phone tour site
  Fort Scott Chamber of Commerce
  Kansas Tourism

- "Other" source of information (1%) was:

  Signs

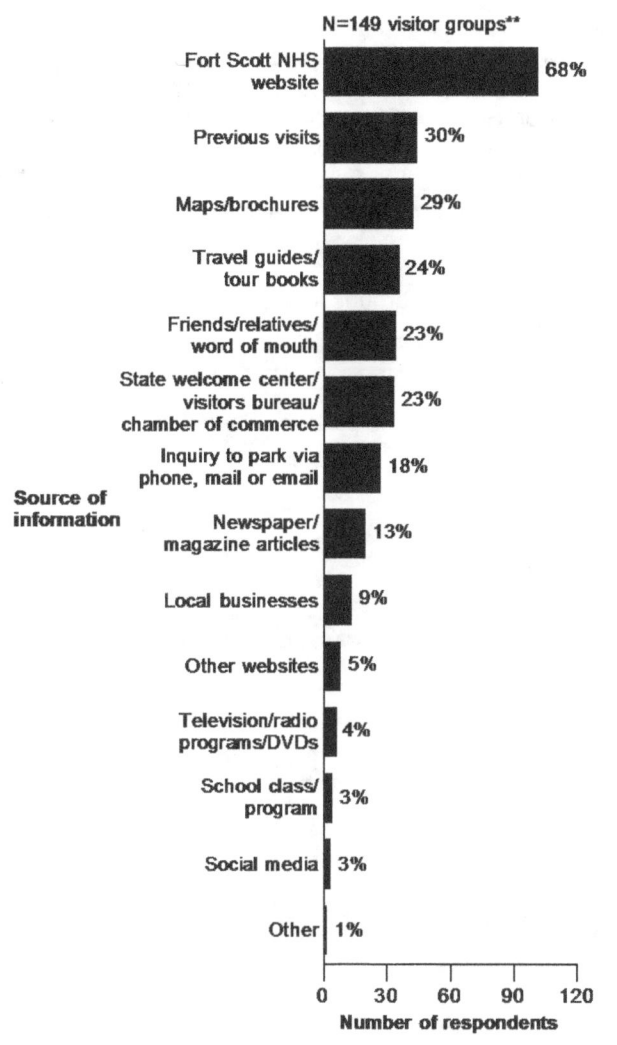

Figure 21. Sources of information to use for a future visit

---

*total percentages do not equal 100 due to rounding

**total percentages do not equal 100 because visitors could select more than one answer

Park as destination

Question from on-site interview

A two-minute interview was conducted with each individual selected to complete the Fort Scott NHS questionnaire. During the interview, the question was asked: "How did this visit to Fort Scott NHS fit into your personal group's travel plans?"

Results

- 41% of visitor groups indicated the park was not a planned destination (see Figure 22).

- 30% indicated the park was their primary destination.

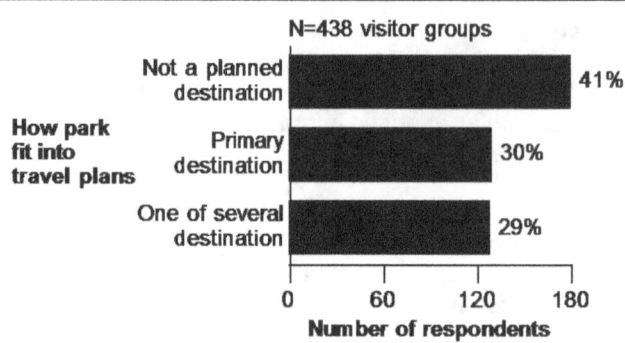

Figure 22. How visit to park fit into visitor groups' travel plans

---

*total percentages do not equal 100 due to rounding

**total percentages do not equal 100 because visitors could select more than one answer

Primary reason for visiting the city of Fort Scott, KS

Question 3

On this trip, what was the primary reason that you and your personal group came to the city of Fort Scott, KS?

Results

- 3% of visitor groups were residents of Fort Scott, KS (see Figure 23).

- As shown in Figure 24, the primary reasons for visiting Fort Scott, KS among non-resident visitor groups were:

  42% Visit the park
  31% Traveling through – unplanned visit
  11% Visit friends/relatives in the area

- "Other" primary reasons (7%) were:

  Genealogy
  Accompanied friends who attended a museum curators meeting in Fort Scott
  Anniversary get-away
  Brought grandkids for second visit
  Camping trip
  Civil War interests
  Family reunion
  Grandmother's birthplace
  Lyons Bed and Breakfast, park, and other attractions
  Motorcycle Poker Run
  National Cemetery
  Paying truck payment
  Read about it in the tourism book
  Rest and relax
  Shopping
  Spent the night in Fort Scott on longer trip
  Stay at Lyons Twin Mansion Bed and Breakfast
  Took granddaughter on tour
  Traveling through - planned
  Visiting relatives in Fort Leavenworth and driving south to Oklahoma City
  Welcome center booklet

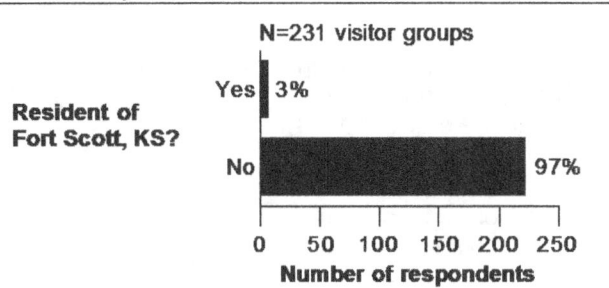

Figure 23. Residents of Fort Scott, KS

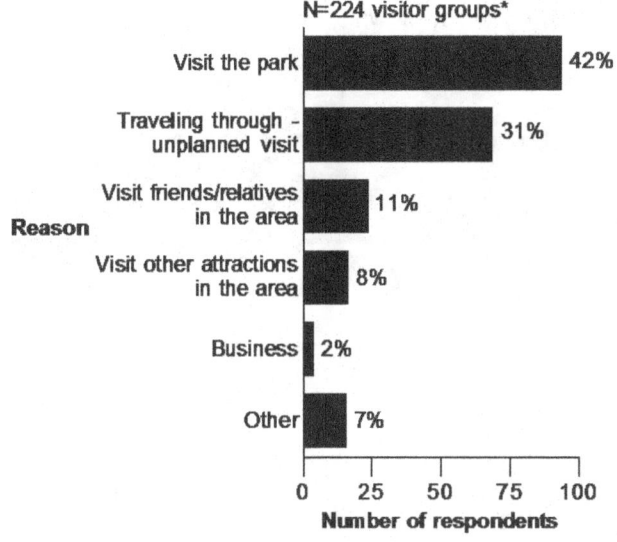

Figure 24. Primary reason for visiting Fort Scott, KS

---

*total percentages do not equal 100 due to rounding
**total percentages do not equal 100 because visitors could select more than one answer

Local and regional attractions visited

Question 4

Which other local and regional attractions did you and your personal group visit on this trip to Fort Scott NHS?

Results

- 63% of visitor groups visited other local and regional attractions (see Figure 25).

- As shown in Figure 26, the most commonly visited local and regional attractions by visitor groups were:

   63% Downtown Fort Scott
   26% Fort Scott National Cemetery
   19% Mine Creek Battlefield

- The least visited attraction was:

   4% Gordon Parks Center

- "Other" attractions (24%) visited are shown in Table 11.

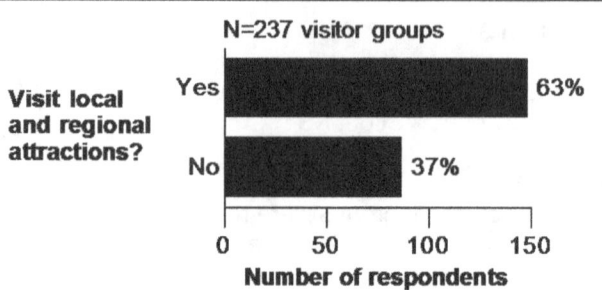

Figure 25. Visitor groups that visited other local regional attractions

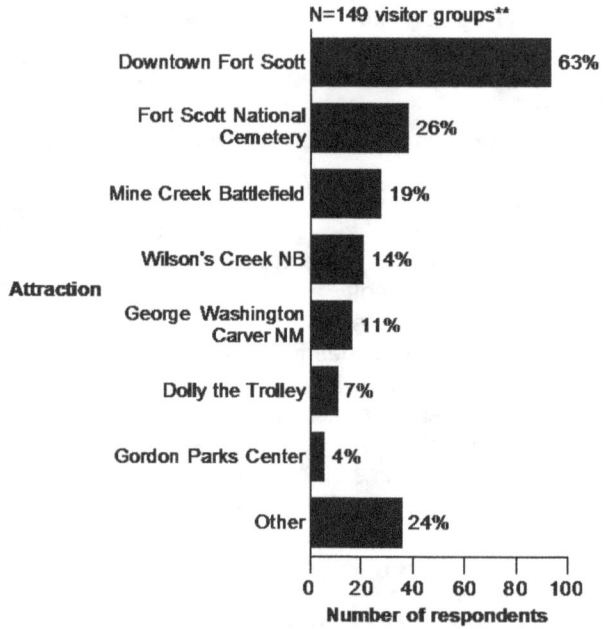

Figure 26. Other local and regional attractions visited

---

*total percentages do not equal 100 due to rounding
**total percentages do not equal 100 because visitors could select more than one answer

Table 11. Other local and regional attractions visited
(N=40 attractions)

Attractions	Number of times mentioned
Big Brutus, West Mineral, KS	5
Marais des Cygnes Massacre site	5
Pea Ridge National Battlefield	3
Genealogy Society	2
Lyons Twin Mansion	2
Truman Birthplace State Historic Site, Lamar, MO	2
Branson, MO	1
Bushwhacker Museum, Nevada, MO	1
Church - First Baptist, daily stops	1
Courtland Hotel	1
Crawford State Park Campground	1
Fort Larned NHS	1
Fort Scott Lake	1
Fort Scott Presbyterian Church	1
Fort Smith NHS	1
Galena, KS - Four Women on the Route "Tow Tater"	1
George Washington Carver NM	1
Gunn Park, Fort Scott, KS	1
JD's Bar	1
Joplin, MO	1
Lyons House Bed and Breakfast for lunch	1
Nicodemus NHS	1
Nu Grille Cafe	1
Precious Moments Chapel	1
Sutler of Fort Scott	1
Tall grass prairie	1
Tallman Homestead	1

*total percentages do not equal 100 due to rounding
**total percentages do not equal 100 because visitors could select more than one answer

Places stayed on night before visiting the park

Question 6a

On this trip, where did you and your personal group stay on the night before visiting Fort Scott NHS?

Results

- 220 visitor groups listed where they stayed on the night before visiting Fort Scott NHS (see Table 12).

Table 12. Places stayed on the night before visiting Fort Scott NHS (N=116 places)

Place	Number of times mentioned
Fort Scott, KS	13
Overland Park, KS	13
Pittsburg, KS	10
Topeka, KS	10
Joplin, MO	9
Kansas City, MO	8
Branson, MO	6
Nevada, MO	6
Lamar, MO	5
Kansas City, KS	4
Springfield, MO	4
Wichita, KS	4
Carthage, MO	3
Independence, MO	3
Baldwin City, KS	2
Chanute, KS	2
Eureka Springs, AR	2
Girard, KS	2
Iola, KS	2
Lake of the Ozark, MO	2
Lawrence, KS	2
Leawood, KS	2
Lincoln, NE	2
Manhattan, KS	2
Mound City, KS	2
Neosho, MO	2
Oklahoma City, OK	2
Olathe, KS	2
Osage Beach, MO	2
Parsons, KS	2
Pleasanton, KS	2
Pratt, KS	2
Redfield, KS	2
Salina, KS	2
Shawnee, KS	2
Ash Grove, MO	1
Baxter Springs, KS	1
Bellavista, unspecified state	1
Bellevue, NE	1
Bentonville, AR	1

*total percentages do not equal 100 due to rounding

**total percentages do not equal 100 because visitors could select more than one answer

Table 12. Places stayed on the night before visiting Fort Scott NHS (continued)

Place	Number of times mentioned
Berryton, KS	1
Berryville, AR	1
Big Spring NP, MO	1
Blue Springs, MO	1
Bolivar, MO	1
Bridgeport, CT	1
Burlington, KS	1
Caldwell, KS	1
Clay Center, KS	1
Columbia, MO	1
Columbus, KS	1
Cushing, OK	1
Dodge City, KS	1
El Dorado, KS	1
Eldorado Springs, MO	1
Emporia, KS	1
Eureka, KS	1
Fayetteville, AR	1
Festus, MO	1
Fort Gibson, OK	1
Gardner, KS	1
Gladstone, MO	1
Goddard, KS	1
Greenwood, IN	1
Grove, OK	1
Independence, MD	1
Ionia, MO	1
Jefferson City, MO	1
Kearney, MO	1
La Cygne, KS	1
La Junta, CO	1
Laclede, MO	1
Lake Cheney, KS	1
Leavenworth, KS	1
Leland, IA	1
Leoti, KS	1
Liberal, MO	1
Little Rock, AR	1
Louisburg, KS	1
Lyndon, KS	1
McCune, KS	1
Meriden, KS	1
Muscogee, OK	1
New Florence, MO	1
Newton, IA	1
Nixa, MO	1

*total percentages do not equal 100 due to rounding
**total percentages do not equal 100 because visitors could select more than one answer

Table 12 Places stayed on the night before visiting Fort Scott NHS (continued)

Place	Number of times mentioned
Oak Grove, MO	1
Odessa, MO	1
Paola, KS	1
Pea Ridge, AK	1
Pierce City, MO	1
Piney River, MO	1
Pleasant Hill, MO	1
Poplar Bluff, MO	1
Rich Hill, MO	1
Roeland Park, KS	1
Saginaw, MO	1
Saint Charles, MO	1
Saint Clair, MO	1
Sapulpa, OK	1
Springfield, IL	1
Stark, KS	1
Stillwater, OK	1
Stockton, MO	1
Sunrise Beach, MO	1
Tecumseh, KS	1
Tonganoxie, KS	1
Tunas, MO	1
Uniontown, KS	1
Unspecified, KS	1
Unspecified, NE	1
Valley Center, KS	1
Webb City, MO	1
Williamstown, NJ	1
Wright, KS	1

*total percentages do not equal 100 due to rounding
**total percentages do not equal 100 because visitors could select more than one answer

Places stayed on night after visiting the park

Question 6b

On this trip, where did you and your personal group stay on the night after visiting Fort Scott NHS?

Results

- 216 visitor groups listed where they stayed on the night after visiting Fort Scott NHS (see Table 13).

Table 13. Places stayed on the night after visiting Fort Scott NHS (N=130 places)

Place	Number of times mentioned
Fort Scott, KS	11
Overland Park, KS	8
Topeka, KS	8
Branson, MO	7
Joplin, MO	7
Wichita, KS	7
Kansas City, MO	6
Springfield, MO	6
Nevada, MO	5
Pittsburg, KS	5
Carthage, MO	4
Bentonville, AR	3
El Dorado, KS	3
Iola, KS	3
Pleasanton, KS	3
Baxter Springs, KS	2
Columbia, MO	2
Council Grove, KS	2
Des Moines, IA	2
Dodge City, KS	2
Garden City, KS	2
Gardner, KS	2
Girard, KS	2
Kansas City, KS	2
Lebanon, MO	2
Mound City, KS	2
Nixa, MO	2
Olathe, KS	2
Redfield, KS	2
Rogers, AR	2
Tulsa, OK	2
Unspecified, KS	2
Ames, IA	1
Argyle, TX	1
Ash Grove, MO	1
Babler Memorial State Park, MO	1
Baldwin City, KS	1

*total percentages do not equal 100 due to rounding
**total percentages do not equal 100 because visitors could select more than one answer

Table 13. Places stayed on the night after visiting Fort Scott NHS (continued)

Place	Number of times mentioned
Basehor, KS	1
Belton, MO	1
Berryton, KS	1
Berryville, AR	1
Bolivar, MO	1
Buffalo Point Campground, AR	1
Buffalo River, AR	1
Caldwell, KS	1
Cameron, MO	1
Chanute, KS	1
Charleston, MO	1
Clay Center, KS	1
Cottonwood Falls, KS	1
Council Bluffs, IA	1
Dallas, TX	1
Denver, CO	1
El Dorado State Park, KS	1
Emporia, KS	1
Falls City, NE	1
Fort Smith, AR	1
Garland, TX	1
Goddard, KS	1
Great Bend, KS	1
Hardin, MO	1
Home Parts, AR	1
Hutchinson, KS	1
Independence, MO	1
Ionia, MO	1
Jefferson City, MO	1
Joplin, MO	1
Kansas City, unspecified state	1
Kingdom City, MO	1
La Cygne, KS	1
Lake of the Ozarks, MO	1
Lamar, MO	1
Lansing, KS	1
Leavenworth, KS	1
Leland, IA	1
Liberal, MO	1
Limon, CO	1
Lincoln, NE	1
Little Rock, AR	1
Louisburg, KS	1
Lyndon, KS	1
Manhattan, KS	1
McPherson, KS	1

*total percentages do not equal 100 due to rounding
**total percentages do not equal 100 because visitors could select more than one answer

Table 13. Places stayed on the night after visiting Fort Scott NHS (continued)

Place	Number of times mentioned
Memphis, TN	1
Miami, OK	1
Monkey Island, OK	1
Mountain View, MO	1
Nebraska City, NE	1
Newton, IA	1
Newton, KS	1
Oak Grove, MO	1
Odessa, MO	1
Oklahoma City, OK	1
Omaha, NE	1
Osage Beach, MO	1
Palmyra, NE	1
Papillion, NE	1
Paris, TX	1
Park City, KS	1
Parsons, KS	1
Peasant Hill, MO	1
Pierce City, MO	1
Prairie Village, KS	1
Rich Hill, MO	1
Roeland Park, KS	1
Saint Charles, MO	1
Saint Paul, KS	1
Salina, KS	1
San Antonio, TX	1
Sapulpa, OK	1
Sedalia, MO	1
Seward, NE	1
Shawnee, KS	1
Siloam Springs, AR	1
Sioux City, IA	1
Springfield, IL	1
Stark, KS	1
Strafford, MO	1
Sunrise Beach, MO	1
Tecumseh, KS	1
Thornburg, KS	1
Uniontown, KS	1
Unspecified, WI	1
Waverly, KS	1
Webb City, MO	1
West Memphis, AR	1
Whitesboro, TX	1
Winfield, KS	1

*total percentages do not equal 100 due to rounding
**total percentages do not equal 100 because visitors could select more than one answer

Services used in nearby communities

Question 9a

In which communities did you and your personal group obtain support services (e.g. information, gas, food, lodging) for this visit to Fort Scott NHS?

Results

- 54% of visitor groups needed support services on this visit (see Figure 27).

- As shown in Figure 28, the communities most commonly used to obtain support services were:

  66% Fort Scott, KS
  19% Pittsburg, KS
  16% Nevada, MO

- "Other" communities (19%) were:

  Carthage, MO
  El Dorado, KS
  Eureka, KS
  Girard, KS
  Independence, MO
  Jefferson City, MO
  Joliet MO
  Joplin, MO
  Kansas City, MO
  Kansas City, unspecified state
  Kearney, MO
  Lamar, MO
  Moran, KS
  Paola, KS
  Parsons, KS
  Perry, OK
  Pleasanton, KS
  Scammon, KS
  Topeka, KS
  Uniontown, KS
  Wichita, KS

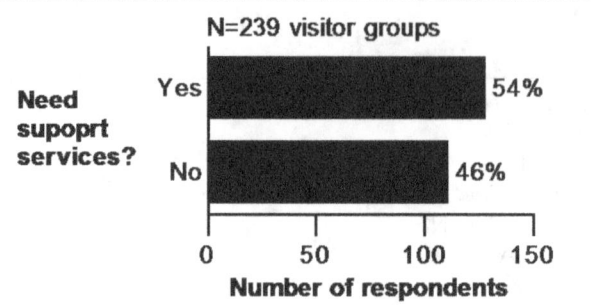

Figure 27. Visitor groups that needed support services on this visit

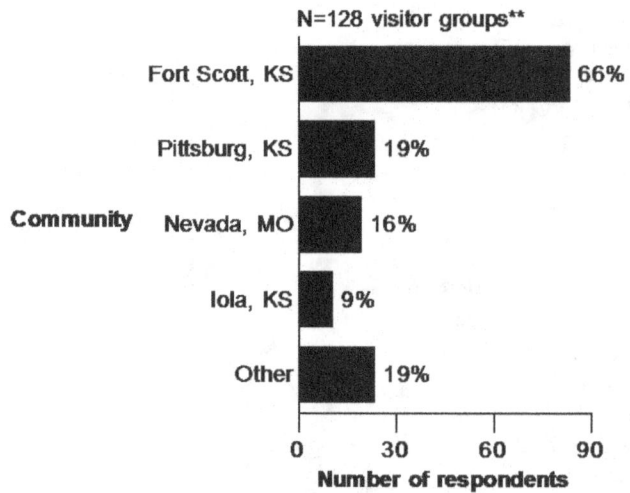

Figure 28. Nearby communities in which visitor groups obtained support services

_____
*total percentages do not equal 100 due to rounding
**total percentages do not equal 100 because visitors could select more than one answer

Question 9b
Were you and your personal group able to obtain all the services that you needed in these communities?

Results
- 96% of visitor groups were able to obtain needed support services in nearby communities (see Figure 29).

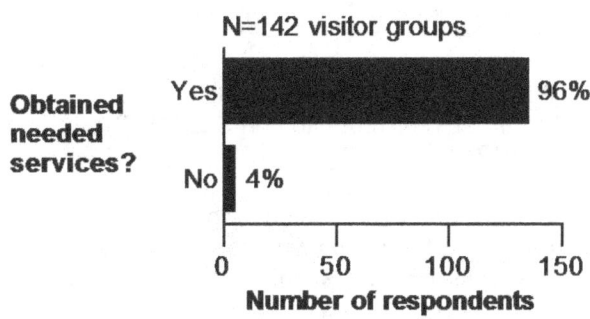

Figure 29. Visitor groups that were able to obtain needed services

Question 9c
If NO, what services were not available? (Open-ended)

Results – Interpret results with **CAUTION!**
- Three visitor groups responded to this question, which is insufficient data to provide reliable results (see Table 14).

Table 14. Needed services that were not available (N=3 comments) – **CAUTION!**

Service	Comment	Number of times mentioned
Groceries	We were looking for a grocery store	1
Hotel	All were full so we had to go to town in Missouri	1
Trolley	Only on weekends - we were here Monday	1

*total percentages do not equal 100 due to rounding
**total percentages do not equal 100 because visitors could select more than one answer

Adequacy of directional signs

Questions 8a and 8b

On this visit, were the signs directing you and your personal group to Fort Scott NHS adequate?

Results

- Table 15 shows visitor groups' ratings of the adequacy of signs directing them to the park.

Table 15. Adequacy of directional signs
(N=number of visitor groups that responded to the question;
n_1=number of visitor groups that rated adequacy of signs;
n_2=number of visitor groups that did not use signs)

Sign	Total N	n_1	Adequate? (%)* Yes	No	n_2	Did not use % of total
a. Regional highway signs	243	205	96	4	38	16
b. City street signs	237	206	96	4	31	13

Question 8c

If you answered NO to either of the above, please explain the problem. (Open-ended)

Results – Interpret results with **CAUTION!**

- 13 visitor groups responded to this question, which is insufficient data to provide reliable data (see Table 16).

Table 16. Problems with directional signs – **CAUTION!**
(N=18 comments; some visitor groups made more than one comment)

Sign	Comment	Number of times mentioned
Regional highway signs	Did not see any directional signs	5
	Could not find correct exit number from a connecting road	1
	Exit from 69 North was confusing	1
	Not marked well in advance	1
	We came in from 69 South and did not see any signs. We used GPS to make sure we were on the correct route.	1
City street signs	Did not see directional signs to park	4
	Did not see the park and ended up roaming through town looking for Fort Scott	1
	Didn't see an signs for fort, just Historical Site #1	1
	Difficult time going back to highway	1
	For cemetery only	1
	Signs need to be placed on the edge of the city limits and not just near the fort. I wasn't sure if I was headed in the right direction.	1

---

*total percentages do not equal 100 due to rounding
**total percentages do not equal 100 because visitors could select more than one answer

Forms of transportation

Question 7a

On this visit, which forms of transportation did you and your group use to travel between your overnight accommodations or home and Fort Scott NHS?

Results

- As shown in Figure 30, the forms of transportation most commonly used to travel between visitor groups' overnight accommodations or home and the park were:

    91% Private vehicle
    6% Rental vehicle

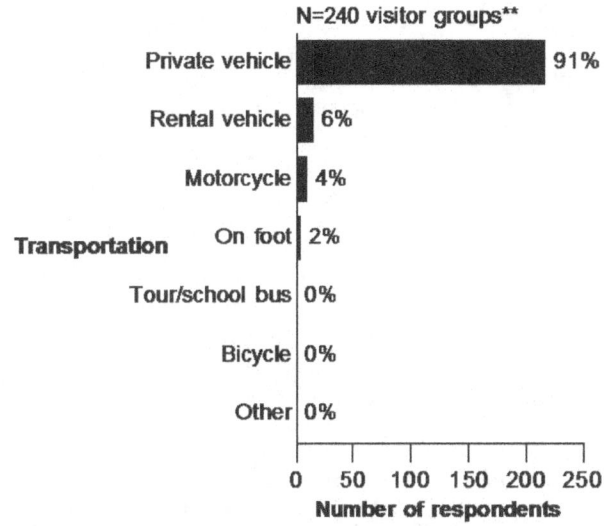

Figure 30. Forms of transportation

Question 7b

On this visit, how many vehicles did you and your personal group use to arrive at the park?

Results

- 93% of visitor groups used one vehicle (see Figure 31).

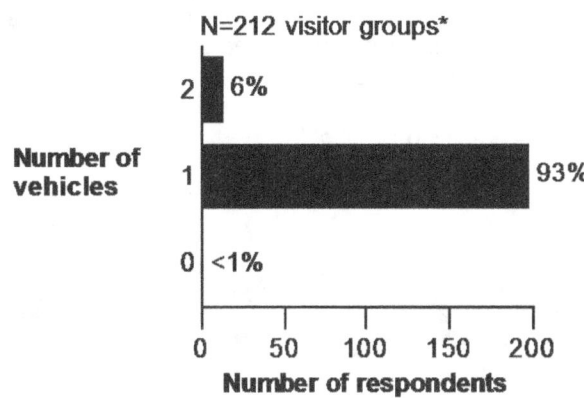

Figure 31. Number of vehicles

Question 24c

How many times did you and your personal group enter Fort Scott NHS on this visit?

Results

- 93% of visitor groups entered the park once (see Figure 32).

- 6% entered two times.

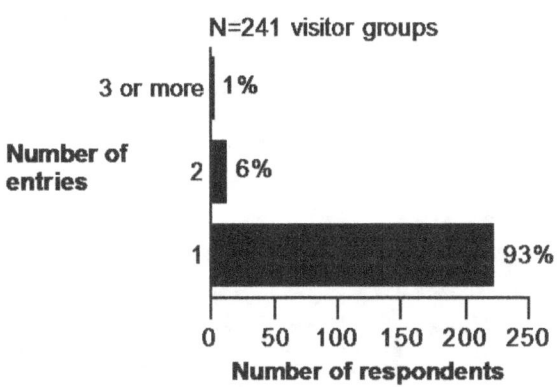

Figure 32. Number of park entries

---

*total percentages do not equal 100 due to rounding
**total percentages do not equal 100 because visitors could select more than one answer

Overnight stays

Question 5a

On this trip, did you and your personal group stay overnight away from your permanent residence in Fort Scott, KS?

Results

- 18% of visitor groups stayed overnight away from home in Fort Scott, KS (see Figure 33).

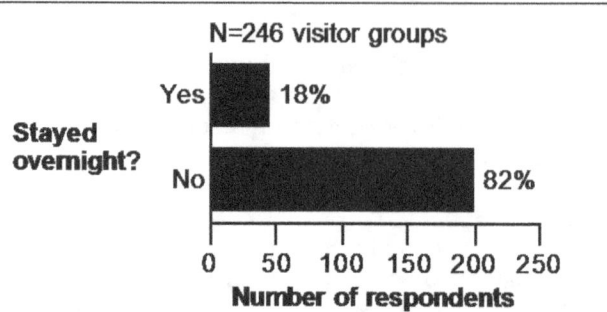

Figure 33. Visitor groups that stayed overnight in Fort Scott, KS

Question 5b

If YES, please list the number of nights you and your personal group stayed in Fort Scott, KS.

Results

- 60% of visitor groups stayed one night in Fort Scott, KS (see Figure 34).

- 24% stayed two nights.

- 17% stayed three or more nights.

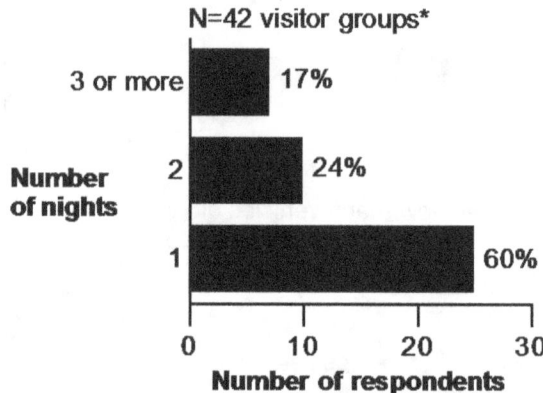

Figure 34. Number of nights spent in Fort Scott, KS

---

*total percentages do not equal 100 due to rounding
**total percentages do not equal 100 because visitors could select more than one answer

Accommodations used in Fort Scott, KS

Question 5c

In which type(s) of lodging did you and your personal group spend the night(s) in Fort Scott, KS?

Results

- As shown in Figure 35, among those visitor groups that stayed overnight in Fort Scott, KS, the most common types of accommodations were:

  67% Lodges, hotels, motels, vacation rentals, B&B, etc.
  21% Residence of friends or relatives
  16% RV/trailer camping

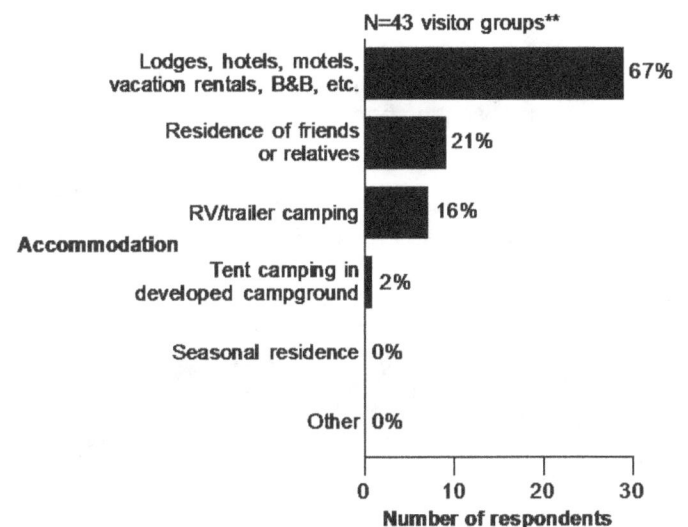

Figure 35. Accommodations used in Fort Scott, KS

---

*total percentages do not equal 100 due to rounding

**total percentages do not equal 100 because visitors could select more than one answer

Length of visit

Question 16a

On this visit to Fort Scott NHS, how much time in total did you and your personal group spend visiting the park?

Results

- 50% of visitor groups spent two hours visiting the park (see Figure 36).

- 38% spent up to one hour.

- 11% spent three or more hours.

- The average length of visit was 1.6 hours.

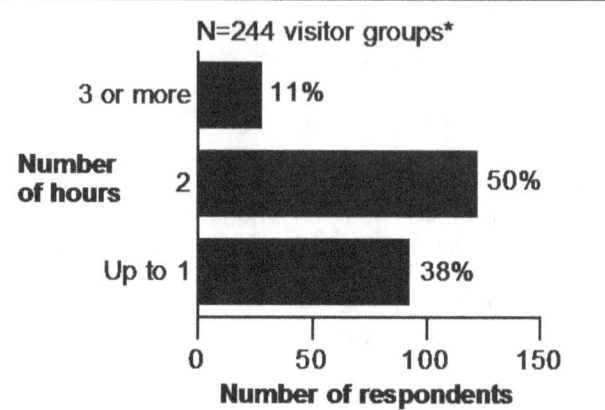

Figure 36. Number of hours spent in the park

Visit the park on more than one day

Question 16b

Did you and your personal group visit the park on more than one day?

Results

- 2% of visitor groups visited the park on more than one day (see Figure 37).

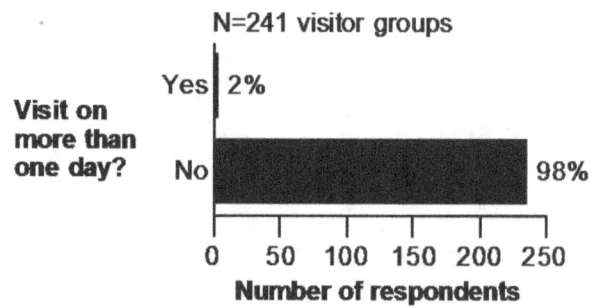

Figure 37. Visitor groups that visited the park on more than one day

Question 16c

If YES, how many days?

Results – Interpret results with **CAUTION!**

- Not enough visitor groups responded to this question to provide reliable results (see Figure 38).

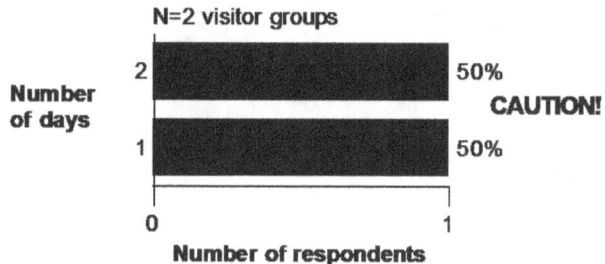

Figure 38. Number of days spent visiting the park

---

*total percentages do not equal 100 due to rounding
**total percentages do not equal 100 because visitors could select more than one answer

Activities on this visit

Question 13a

On this visit, in which activities did you and your personal group participate within Fort Scott NHS?

Results

- As shown in Figure 39, the most common activities in which visitor groups participated on this visit were:

    85% General sightseeing
    83% Viewing indoor exhibits and furnished rooms
    82% Viewing outdoor exhibits and buildings

- "Other" activities (10%) were:

    Educational
    General interest in site
    Historical and ranger programs
    Introduce kids to park
    Junior Ranger program
    Learned about history
    Learned military history
    Obtain National Park Passport stamp
    Obtain volunteer information
    Observe the building methods
    Stretch legs during car ride

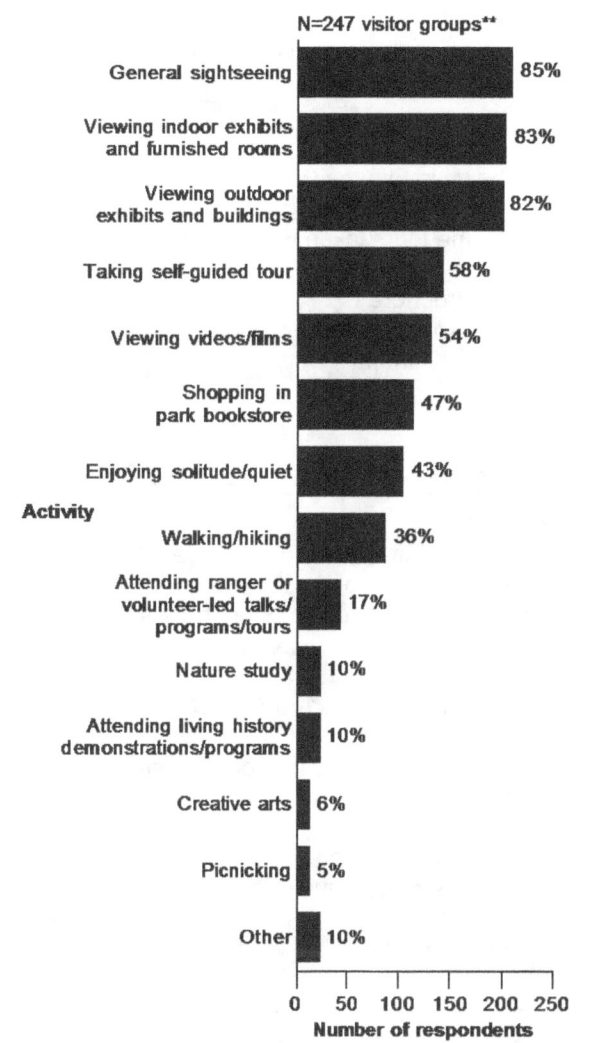

Figure 39. Activities on this visit

---

*total percentages do not equal 100 due to rounding
**total percentages do not equal 100 because visitors could select more than one answer

Self-guided tour of fort

Question 13a
Which self-guided tour did you and your personal group take?

Results
- As shown in Figure 40, of the visitor groups that took a self-guided tour (58%), the tours taken were:

  82% Brochure
  10% Brochure and cell phone
   8% Cell phone

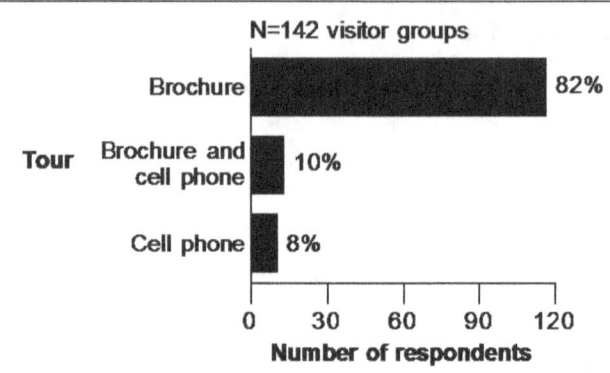

Figure 40. Self-guided tour

Activity that was primary reason for visiting the park

Question 13b
Which one of the above activities was the primary reason you and your personal group visited Fort Scott NHS on this visit?

Results
- As shown in Figure 41, the most common activities that visitor groups listed as their primary reason for visiting the park were:

  53% General sightseeing
  10% Taking self-guided tour

- "Other" activities (12%) were:

  Educational
  General interest in site
  Historical and ranger programs
  Introduce kids to park
  Learned about history
  Learned military history
  Obtain National Park Passport stamp
  Obtain volunteer information
  Observe the building methods
  Stretch legs during car ride

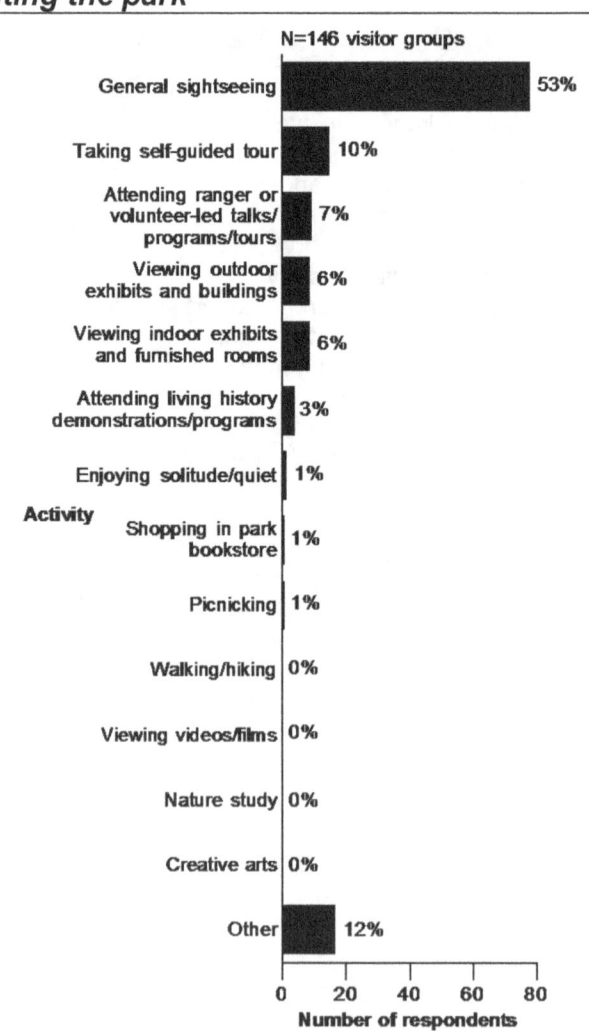

Figure 41. Activity that was primary reason for visiting the park

---

*total percentages do not equal 100 due to rounding
**total percentages do not equal 100 because visitors could select more than one answer

Ranger or volunteer-led talks, programs, or tours

Question 10a

On this visit to Fort Scott NHS, did anyone in your personal group participate in any of the ranger or volunteer-led talks/programs/tours?

Results

- 28% of visitor groups participated in ranger or volunteer-led talks, programs, or tours (see Figure 42).

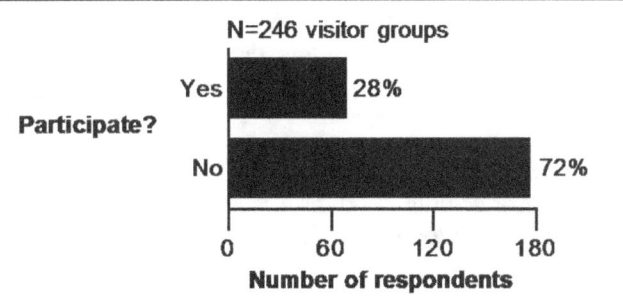

Figure 42. Visitor groups that participated in ranger or volunteer-led talks, programs, or tours

Question 10b

If NO, what prevented you and your personal group from participating in ranger or volunteer-led talks/programs/tours?

Results

- As shown in Figure 43, the most common reasons preventing visitor groups from participating in ranger or volunteer-led talks, programs, or tours were:

    53% Did not have time for this activity
    29% Programs not offered at time of visit
    12% Not interested

- "Other" reasons (15%) were:

    Dad is historian, he did a lot of the "informing"
    Got all the information I needed from volunteer
    Heat
    History information
    Preferred self-guided cellphone tour
    Preferred self-guided tour
    Previous knowledge
    Raining
    Read information prior to visit
    Schedule
    Sightseeing
    Watched 20 minute video

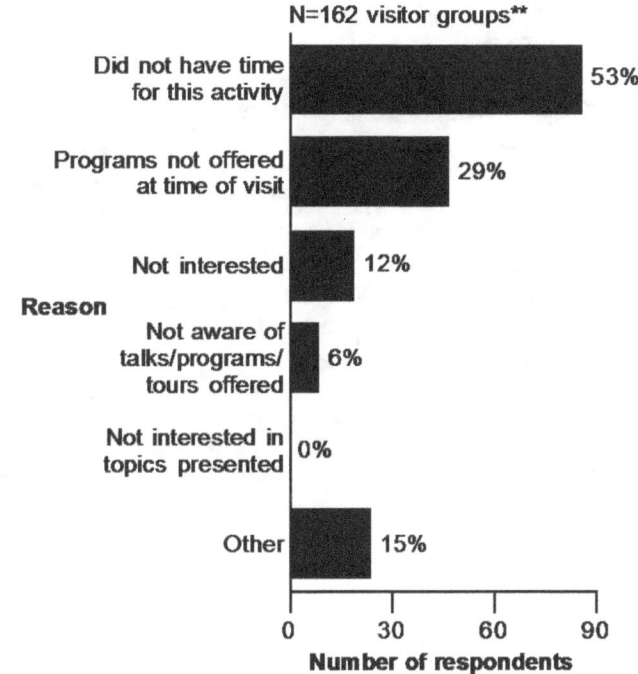

Figure 43. Reasons for not participating in ranger or volunteer-led talks, programs, or tours

---

*total percentages do not equal 100 due to rounding
**total percentages do not equal 100 because visitors could select more than one answer

Question 15a
On this visit, which ranger or volunteer-led talks/programs/tours, if any, did you attend?

Results
- 26% of visitor groups attended ranger or volunteer-led talks, programs, or tours (see Figure 44).

- As shown in Figure 45, the talks, programs or tours visitor groups attended were:

    43% Guided tour
    39% Talk
    14% Musical/dramatic/living
        history presentation

- "Other" talks, programs, or tours (9%) were:

    Junior Ranger program
    Overview in bookstore
    Ranger explained park history
        at welcome center

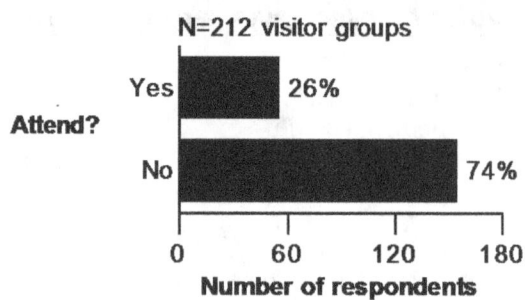

Figure 44. Visitor groups that attended ranger or volunteer-led talks, programs, or tours

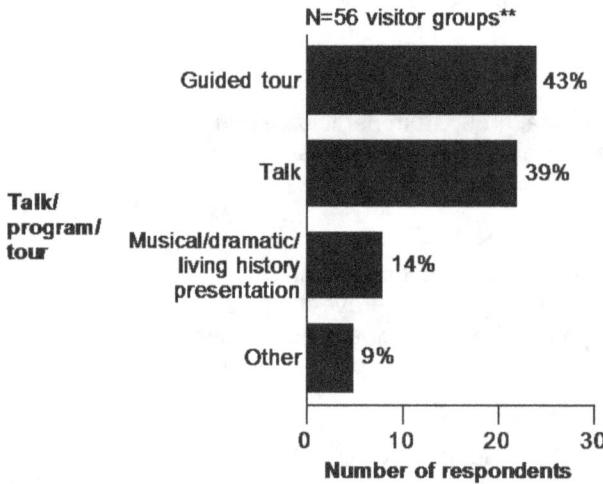

Figure 45. Ranger or volunteer-led talks, programs, or tours

---

*total percentages do not equal 100 due to rounding
**total percentages do not equal 100 because visitors could select more than one answer

Evaluation of ranger or volunteer-led talks, programs, or tours

Question 15b

If you attended more than one talk/program/tour, please choose one to evaluate.

Results

- 41% of visitor groups evaluated the guided tour (see Figure 46).

- 35% evaluated the talk.

- "Other" talks, programs, or tours (9%) were:

  Junior Ranger program
  Overview in gift shop
  Ranger explained park history at welcome center

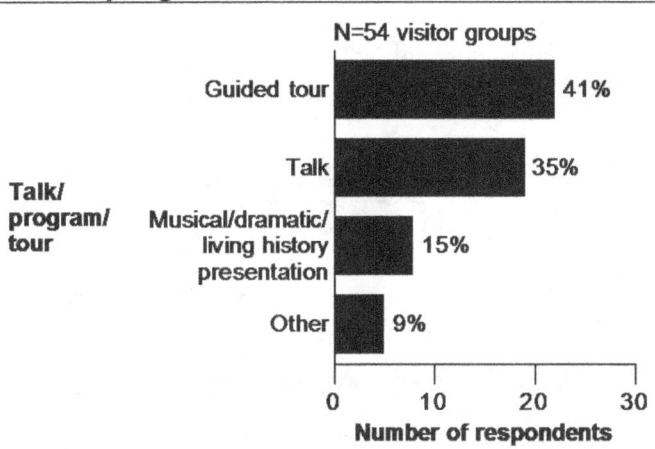

Figure 46. Visitor groups that evaluated ranger or volunteer-led talks, programs, or tours on this visit

Question 15c

Please evaluate the length of the program you attended.

Results – Interpret results with **CAUTION!**

- Not enough visitor groups responded to the question to provide reliable results (see Table 17).

Table 17. Evaluation of program length (N=number of visitor groups) – **CAUTION!**

Talk/program/tour	N	Program length (%)		
		Too short	About right	Too long
Guided tour	19	0	95	5
Talk	18	0	100	0
Musical/dramatic/living history presentation	8	0	100	0
Other	4	0	100	0

Question 15d

Please evaluate the effect of the tour size on your ability to see room interiors for the program you attended.

Results – Interpret results with **CAUTION!**

- Not enough visitor groups responded to the question to provide reliable results (see Table 18).

Table 18. Evaluation of effect of tour size on ability to see room interiors (N=number of visitor groups) – **CAUTION!**

Talk/program/tour	N	Effect of tour size (%)	
		No effect – able to see	Had difficulty seeing
Guided tour	19	100	0
Talk	16	100	0
Musical/dramatic/living history presentation	7	100	0
Other	4	100	0

---

*total percentages do not equal 100 due to rounding
**total percentages do not equal 100 because visitors could select more than one answer

Question 15e
Please indicate whether or not the topics discussed in the program you attended were of interest.

Results – Interpret results with **CAUTION!**
- Not enough visitor groups responded to the question to provide reliable results (see Table 19).

Table 19. Interest in topics discussed (N=number of visitor groups) – **CAUTION!**

Talk/program/tour	N	Interest in topic (%)	
		Of interest	Not of interest
Guided tour	19	100	0
Talk	16	100	0
Musical/dramatic/living history presentation	8	100	0
Other	4	100	0

Question 14a
If you attended a talk, program, or tour on this visit, were you able to hear what the ranger or volunteer was saying?

Results
- 85% of visitor groups were able to hear what was said during a ranger or volunteer-led talk, program or tour (see Figure 47).

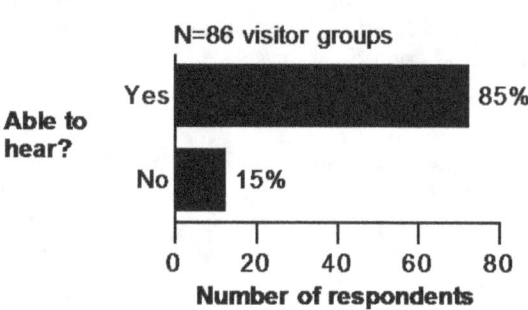

Figure 47. Visitor groups that were able to hear what was said during a ranger or volunteer-led talk, program, or tour

Question 14b
If NO, what was/were the reason(s) for the problem?

Results – Interpret results with **CAUTION!**
- Not enough visitor groups responded to this question to provide reliable results (see Figure 48).

- "Other" reasons (60%) were:

    Didn't have time
    Heat

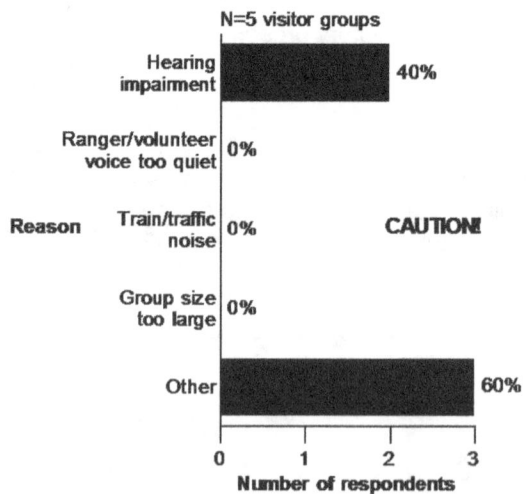

Figure 48. Reasons visitor groups were not able to hear what was said during a ranger or volunteer-led talk, program, or tour

*total percentages do not equal 100 due to rounding
**total percentages do not equal 100 because visitors could select more than one answer

Question 15f

Did you learn something about Fort Scott HNS from the talk/program/tour that is relevant or meaningful to your life today?

Results – Interpret results with **CAUTION!**
- Not enough visitor groups responded to the question to provide reliable results (see Table 20).

Table 20. Visitor groups that learned something meaningful/relevant (N=number of visitor groups) – **CAUTION!**

Talk/program/tour	N	Learned something meaningful or relevant (%)		
		Yes	No	Not sure
Guided tour	18	78	0	22
Talk	18	83	0	17
Musical/dramatic/living history presentation	8	75	0	25
Other	4	50	0	50

Question 11

If you were to attend a ranger or volunteer-led program at Fort Scott NHS, which program length would you prefer?

Results
- 56% of visitor groups preferred a program length of 1/2 - 1 hour (see Figure 49).

- 32% preferred a program length of under 1/2 hour.

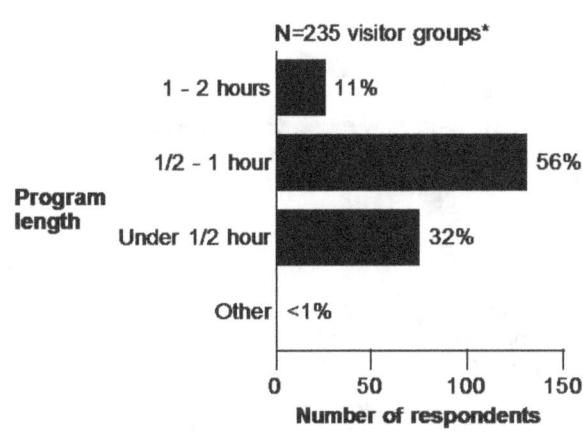

Figure 49. Preferred program length

---

*total percentages do not equal 100 due to rounding
**total percentages do not equal 100 because visitors could select more than one answer

Fort Scott's involvement in historically significant events

Question 19a

Fort Scott NHS was involved in some of the nation's historically significant events. Please indicate all of the historical events that you were aware Fort Scott was involved in.

Results

- Table 21 shows visitor groups' awareness of Fort Scott's involvement in historically significant events.

Table 21. Awareness of Fort Scott's involvement in historically significant events (N=number of visitor groups)

Event	N	Aware (%)	
		Yes	No
Maintaining a permanent Indian frontier	227	37	63
Opening of the West/Westward expansion	229	53	47
"Bleeding" Kansas	224	45	55
Civil War	231	53	47

Question 19b

Please indicate how much your level of understanding of each event improved during your visit.

Results

- 95% of visitor groups learned about Fort Scott's involvement in historically significant events on this visit (see Figure 50).

- Table 22 shows improvement in visitor groups' level of understanding of Fort Scott's involvement in historically significant events on this visit.

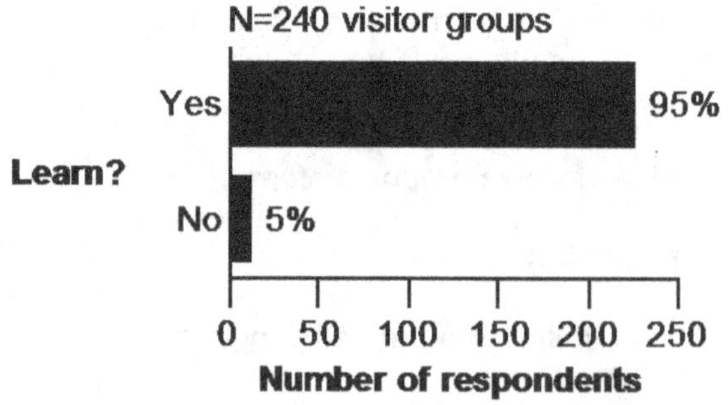

Figure 50. Visitor groups that learned about Fort Scott's involvement in historically significant events on this visit

Table 22. Improvement in level of understanding (N=number of visitor groups)

Event	N	Improvement in level of understanding (%)			
		Not at all	A little	Somewhat	A lot
Maintaining a permanent Indian frontier	220	5	10	29	56
Opening of the West/Westward expansion	222	4	10	32	54
"Bleeding" Kansas	221	5	12	24	59
Civil War	226	2	11	32	55

*total percentages do not equal 100 due to rounding

**total percentages do not equal 100 because visitors could select more than one answer

Question 19c

Next, indicate the events you would be interested in learning (or learning more) about on a future visit.

Results

- Table 23 shows visitor groups' interest in learning about Fort Scott's involvement in historically significant events on a future visit.

Table 23. Interest in learning about Fort Scott's involvement in historically significant events (N=number of visitor groups)

Event	N	Interest in learning (%)	
		Yes	No
Maintaining a permanent Indian frontier	216	86	14
Opening of the West/Westward expansion	213	86	14
"Bleeding" Kansas	213	88	12
Civil War	220	88	12

Question 19d

Please list any aspects of the above events that you and your personal group are interested in learning (or learning more) about during a future visit to Fort Scott NHS. (Open-ended)

Results

- 40 visitor groups listed topics they were interested in learning about.

- Table 24 shows visitor groups' interest in learning about the aspects of Fort Scott's involvement in historically significant events on a future visit.

Table 24. Interest in learning about the aspects of Fort Scott's involvement in historically significant events (N=45 comments; some visitor groups made more than one comment)

Event	Number of times mentioned
Bleeding Kansas	13
Civil War	6
All	2
Care of horses	2
Living conditions and daily routine at fort throughout time	2
Maintaining Indian frontier	2
Women's role during that era	2
Actual battle sites	1
Artillery	1
Children learn importance of western expansion and patriotism	1
Everyday life of soldier/civilian	1
Fort's post-Civil War story	1
Fort's construction history	1
How did they survive	1
How patrolled vast trail	1
More about permanent Indian border	1
Native American history	1
Native American interaction with fort	1
Native American perspectives	1
Opening westward expansion	1
Reenactments	1
Training	1
Underground railroad	1

*total percentages do not equal 100 due to rounding
**total percentages do not equal 100 because visitors could select more than one answer

Ratings of Services, Facilities, Attributes, Resources, and Elements

Information services and facilities used

Question 17a

Please indicate all of the information services and facilities that you or your personal group used at Fort Scott NHS during this visit.

Results

- As shown in Figure 51, the most common information services and facilities used by visitor groups were:

  86% Indoor exhibits
  79% Park brochure/map
  78% Restrooms

- The least used service/facility was:

  4% Access for people with disabilities

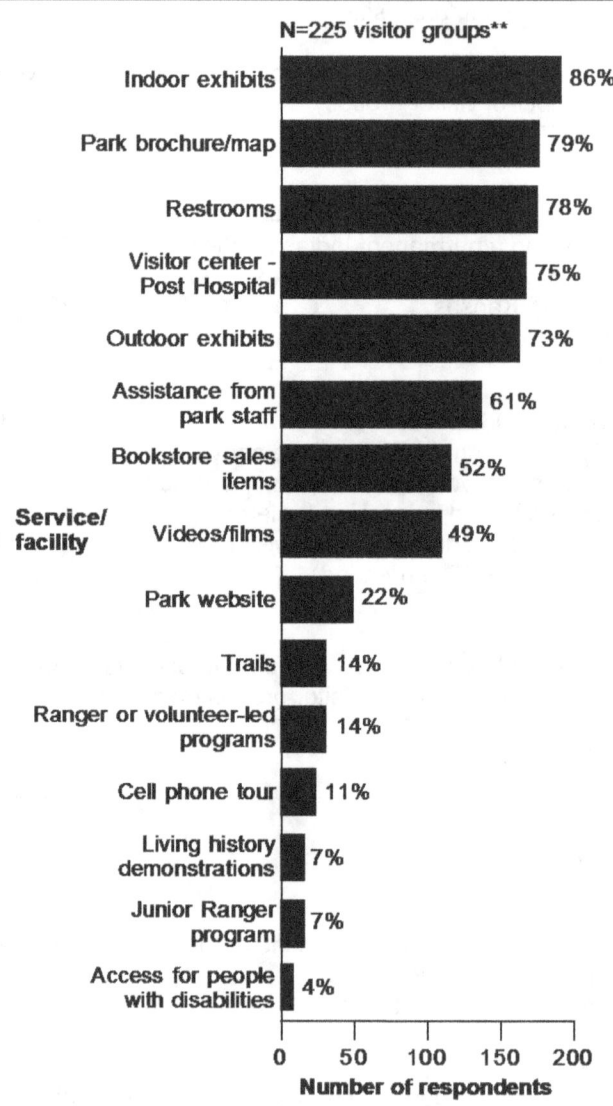

Figure 51. Information services and facilities used

*total percentages do not equal 100 due to rounding
**total percentages do not equal 100 because visitors could select more than one answer

48

Importance ratings of information services and facilities

Question 17b

Next, for only those services and facilities that you or your personal group used, please rate their importance to your visit from 1-5.

1=Not at all important
2=Slightly important
3=Moderately important
4=Very important
5=Extremely important

Results

- Figure 52 shows the combined proportions of "extremely important" and "very important" ratings of information services and facilities that were rated by 30 or more visitor groups.

- The information services and facilities receiving the highest combined proportions of "extremely important" and "very important" ratings were:

  92% Park brochure/map
  91% Indoor exhibits
  90% Visitor center – Post Hospital
  90% Outdoor exhibits

- Table 25 shows the importance ratings of each service and facility.

- The services/facilities receiving the highest "not at all important" rating that were rated by 30 or more visitor groups were:

  1% Bookstore sales items
  1% Indoor exhibits
  1% Park brochure/map
  1% Restrooms
  1% Visitor center – Post Hospital

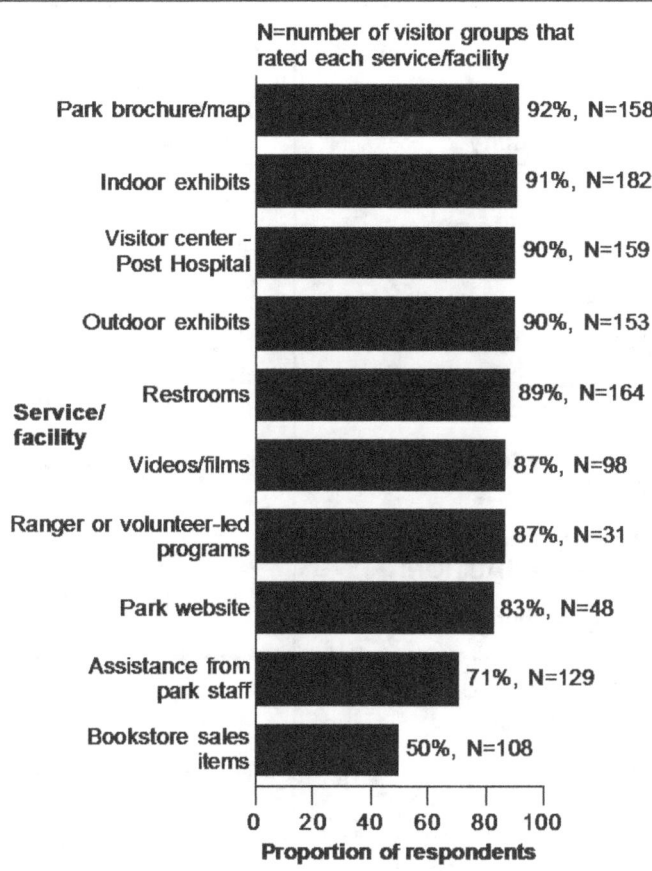

Figure 52. Combined proportions of "extremely important" and "very important" ratings of information services and facilities

---

*total percentages do not equal 100 due to rounding

**total percentages do not equal 100 because visitors could select more than one answer

49

Table 25. Importance ratings of information services and facilities
(N=number of visitor groups that rated each service and facility)

Service/facility	N	Rating (%)*				
		Not at all important	Slightly important	Moderately important	Very important	Extremely important
Access for people with disabilities – **CAUTION!**	6	0	0	17	0	83
Assistance from park staff	129	0	7	22	35	36
Bookstore sales items (selection, price, etc.)	108	1	15	34	27	23
Cell phone tour – **CAUTION!**	23	4	13	17	30	35
Junior Ranger program – **CAUTION!**	15	0	7	20	40	33
Living history demonstrations – **CAUTION!**	16	0	0	19	44	38
Indoor exhibits	182	1	1	8	37	54
Outdoor exhibits	153	0	1	9	34	56
Park brochure/map	158	1	1	6	37	55
Park website used before or during visit	48	0	0	17	31	52
Ranger or volunteer-led programs	31	0	0	13	32	55
Restrooms	164	1	2	8	26	63
Videos/films	98	0	1	12	43	44
Trails – **CAUTION!**	28	0	0	21	32	46
Visitor center – Post Hospital	159	1	2	8	31	59

*total percentages do not equal 100 due to rounding
**total percentages do not equal 100 because visitors could select more than one answer

Quality ratings of information services and facilities

Question 17c

Finally, for only those services and facilities that you or your personal group used, please rate their quality from 1-5.

    1=Very poor
    2=Poor
    3=Average
    4=Good
    5=Very good

Results

- Figure 53 shows the combined proportions of "very good" and "good" ratings of information services and facilities that were rated by 30 or more visitor groups.

- The services and facilities receiving the highest combined proportions of "very good" and "good" ratings were:

    100% Ranger or volunteer-led
        programs
    99% Videos/films
    99% Park brochure/map
    99% Assistance form park staff

- Table 26 shows the quality ratings of each service and facility.

- The service/facility receiving the highest "very poor" rating that was rated by 30 or more visitor groups was:

    1% Park brochure/map

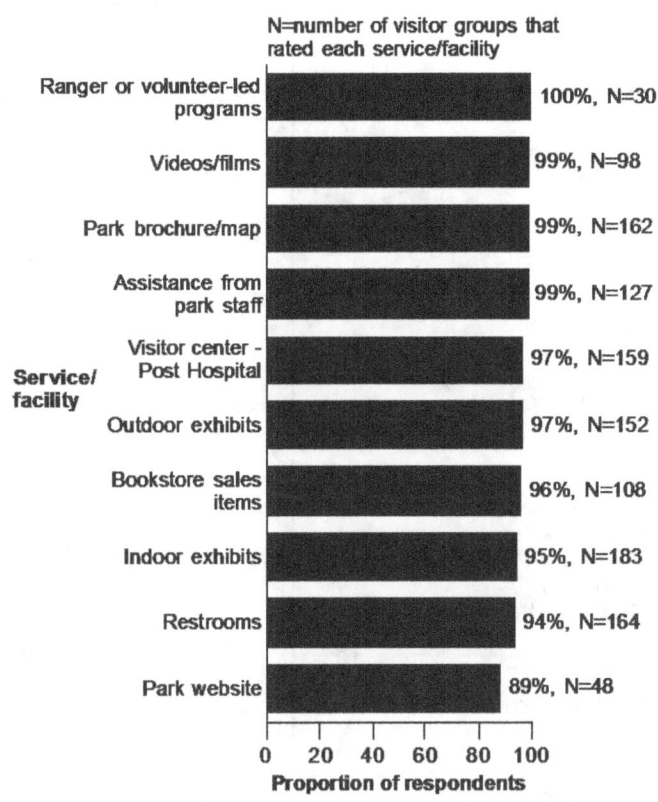

N=number of visitor groups that rated each service/facility

Figure 53. Combined proportions of "very good" and "good" ratings of information services and facilities

---

*total percentages do not equal 100 due to rounding
**total percentages do not equal 100 because visitors could select more than one answer

Table 26. Quality ratings of information services and facilities
(N=number of visitor groups that rated each service and facility)

Service/facility	N	Rating (%)*				
		Very poor	Poor	Average	Good	Very good
Access for people with disabilities – **CAUTION!**	6	0	0	50	0	50
Assistance from park staff	127	0	0	2	19	80
Bookstore sales items (selection, price, etc.)	108	0	0	5	41	55
Cell phone tour – **CAUTION!**	22	0	5	27	18	50
Junior Ranger program – **CAUTION!**	15	0	0	0	33	67
Living history demonstrations – **CAUTION!**	15	0	0	0	33	67
Indoor exhibits	183	0	0	5	29	66
Outdoor exhibits	152	0	0	3	29	68
Park brochure/map	162	1	0	1	30	69
Park website used before or during visit	48	0	0	10	35	54
Ranger or volunteer-led programs	30	0	0	0	23	77
Restrooms	164	0	0	5	27	67
Videos/films	98	0	0	1	29	70
Trails – **CAUTION!**	29	0	0	14	34	52
Visitor center – Post Hospital	159	0	1	3	23	74

*total percentages do not equal 100 due to rounding
**total percentages do not equal 100 because visitors could select more than one answer

Mean scores of importance and quality ratings of information services and facilities

- Figures 54 and 55 show the mean scores of importance and quality ratings of information services and facilities that were rated by 30 or more visitor groups.

- All information services and facilities were rated above average.

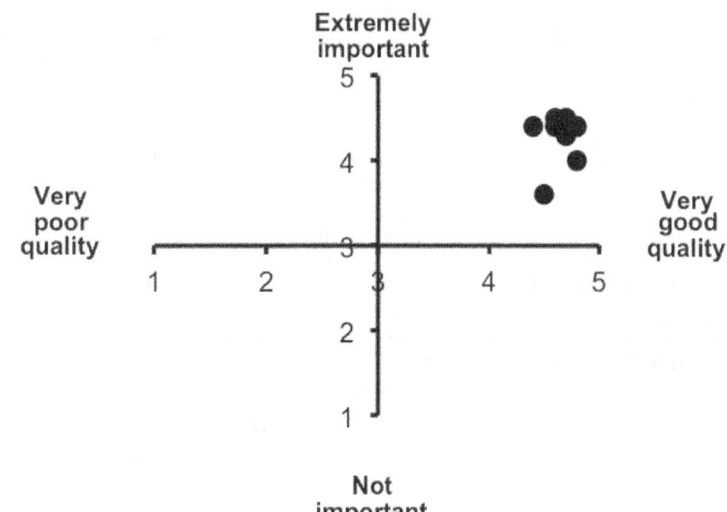

Figure 54. Mean scores of importance and quality of information services and facilities

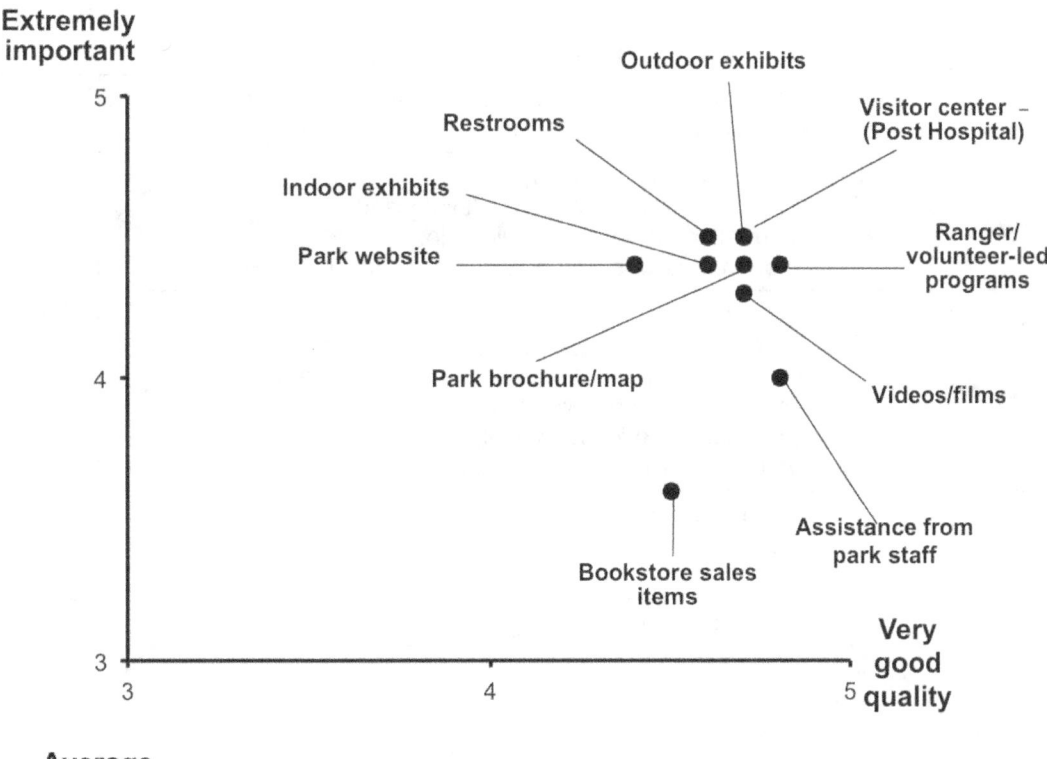

Figure 55. Detail of Figure 54

---

*total percentages do not equal 100 due to rounding
**total percentages do not equal 100 because visitors could select more than one answer

Question 17d

If you and your personal group have comments on any of the above services and facilities, please use the lines below. (Open-ended)

Results

- 41 visitor groups responded to this question.

- Table 27 shows comments on services and facilities.

Table 27. Comments on services and facilities
(N=53 comments; some visitor groups made more than one comment)

Service/facility	Comment	Number of times mentioned
Access for people with disabilities	Did not see or find disability access	1
Assistance from park staff	Staff is friendly	8
	Staff is helpful	6
	Staff is knowledgeable	4
	Level of assistance of ranger and volunteer exhibits high quality	1
	Ranger in visitor center was very awesome and great to our grandsons - made the day!	1
	Staff is caring	1
	We were impressed with the staff and volunteers	1
Cell phone tour	Did not use, but was glad to know it was available. Maybe next time.	1
	Excellent, very convenient	1
Facilities	Impressed by their good maintenance. Air conditioning was very welcome.	1
Indoor exhibits	Extremely well done and informative	1
	Re-created rooms very good. Galleys/posed information dry - video would help.	1
	Very important as was over 100 degrees outside	1
Junior Ranger program	Kept our 2nd grader focused	1
	Perhaps consider limiting the range of the program. It was difficult to complete the assigned number of tasks in the 3 hours we attended. But, it was a very good experience overall.	1
	We love this program. Great for kids.	1
Living history demonstrations	Adds more interest	1
	Would have enjoyed being present on weekend when more was going on	1
Park brochure/map	Should list names of all buildings	1
Park (overall)	Very clean	2
	Easy to use	1
	Very good	1
	Well-maintained	1

*total percentages do not equal 100 due to rounding

**total percentages do not equal 100 because visitors could select more than one answer

Table 27. Comments on services and facilities (continued)

Service/facility	Comment	Number of times mentioned
Park website	Needs more information	1
Ranger or volunteer-led programs	Very enthusiastic and excited about the park	1
Restrooms	Need more	2
	It should be larger	1
	Need improvement	1
	Need one on far side	1
	Needed water	1
	No lock on door for daughter - freaked her out	1
	Only one toilet in ladies' room	1
	Only open in visitor center	1
Stables	Live animals, i.e., blacksmith making wagons, barrels, farrier	1
Videos/films	Very informative	1

*total percentages do not equal 100 due to rounding
**total percentages do not equal 100 because visitors could select more than one answer

Quality of personal interaction with park staff

Question 12a

During this visit to Fort Scott NHS, did you and your personal group have any personal interaction with park staff?

Results
- 94% of visitor groups had interaction with park staff (see Figure 56).

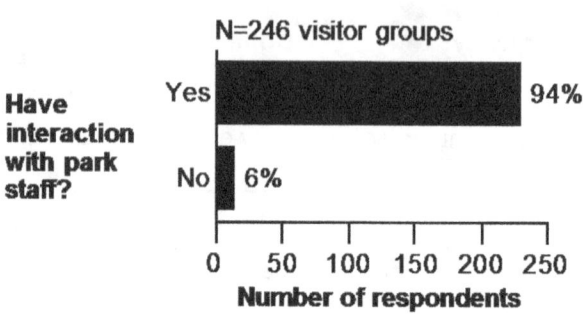

Figure 56. Visitor groups that had interaction with park staff

Question 12b

If YES, please rate the quality of your interaction with park staff.

Results
- Table 28 shows visitor groups' ratings of the quality of interactions with park staff.

Table 28. Quality of personal interaction with park staff
(N=number of visitor groups that rated each element)

Element	N	Rating (%)				
		Very poor	Poor	Average	Good	Very good
Helpfulness	229	1	0	2	15	82
Courteousness	228	1	0	1	12	86
Quality of information provided	227	1	0	1	16	82

*total percentages do not equal 100 due to rounding
**total percentages do not equal 100 because visitors could select more than one answer

Expenditures

Total expenditures inside the park and in Fort Scott, KS

Question 20

For you and your personal group, please estimate all expenditures for the items listed below for this visit to Fort Scott NHS and Fort Scott, KS.

Results

- 35% of visitor groups spent $51 or more on expenditures inside the park and in Fort Scott, KS (see Figure 57).

- 35% spent $1-$50.

- 30% spent no money.

- The average visitor group expenditure was $75.

- The median group expenditure (50% groups spent more and 50% of groups spent less) was $25.

- The average total expenditure per person (per capita) was $35.

- As shown in Figure 58, the largest proportions of total expenditures inside the park and in Fort Scott, KS were:

  25% Lodges, hotels, motels, cabins, B&Bs, etc.
  24% Restaurants and bars
  22% All other purchases
  19% Gas and oil

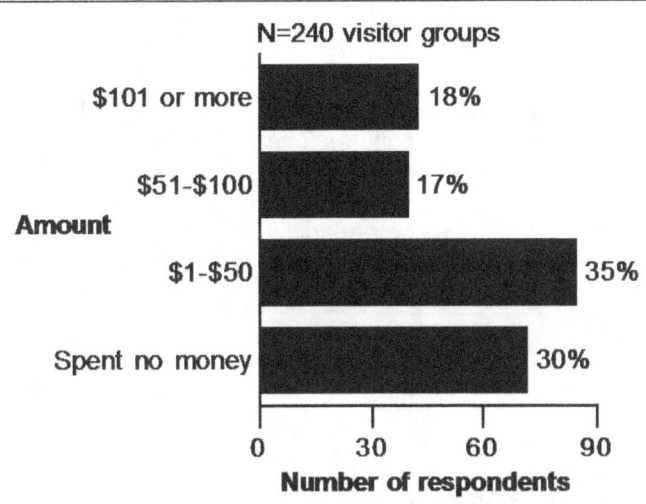

Figure 57. Total expenditures inside the park and in Fort Scott, KS

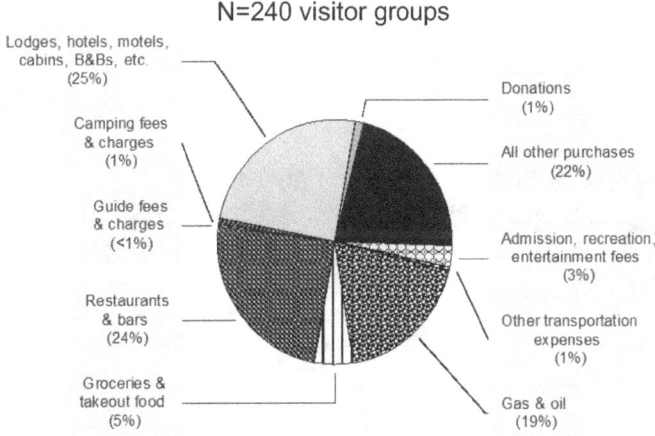

Figure 58. Proportions of total expenditures inside the park and in Fort Scott, KS

---

*total percentages do not equal 100 due to rounding

**total percentages do not equal 100 because visitors could select more than one answer

Number of adults covered by expenditures

Question 20c
How many adults (18 years or older) do these expenses cover?

Results
- 66% of visitor groups had two adults covered by expenditures (see Figure 59).

- 18% had three or more adults covered by expenditures.

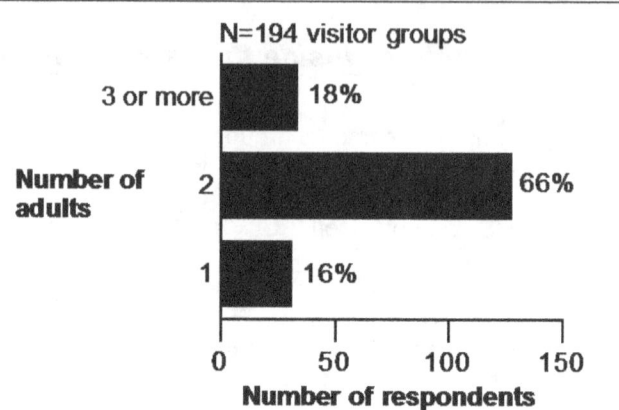

Figure 59. Number of adults covered by expenditures

Number of children covered by expenditures

Question 20c
How many children (under 18 years) do these expenses cover?

Results
- 65% of visitor groups had no children covered by expenditures (see Figure 60).

- 26% had two or more children covered by expenditures.

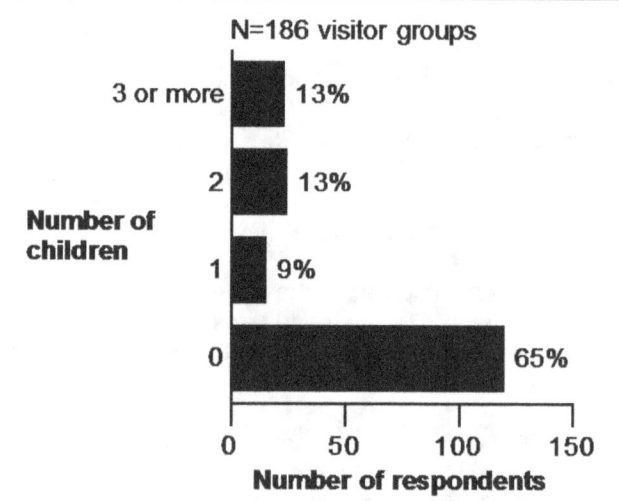

Figure 60. Number of children covered by expenditures

*total percentages do not equal 100 due to rounding
**total percentages do not equal 100 because visitors could select more than one answer

Expenditures inside the park

Question 20a

Please list your group's total expenditures inside Fort Scott NHS.

Results

- 64% of visitor groups spent no money inside the park (see Figure 61).

- 33% spent 1-$50.

- The average visitor group expenditure inside the park was $8.

- The median group expenditure (50% groups spent more and 50% of groups spent less) was $0.

- The average total expenditure per person (per capita) was $11.

- As shown in Figure 62, the largest proportion of total expenditures inside the park was:

  89% All other purchases

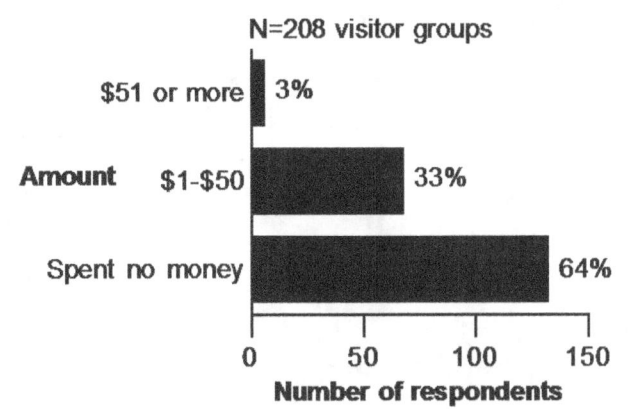

N=208 visitor groups

Figure 61. Total expenditures inside the park

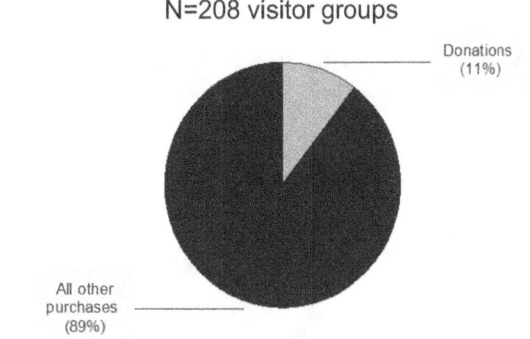

N=208 visitor groups

Figure 62. Proportions of total expenditures inside the park

---

*total percentages do not equal 100 due to rounding
**total percentages do not equal 100 because visitors could select more than one answer

<u>All other purchases</u> (souvenirs, film, books, sporting goods, clothing, etc.)

- 66% of visitor groups spent no money on all other purchases inside the park (see Figure 63).

- 31% spent $1-$50.

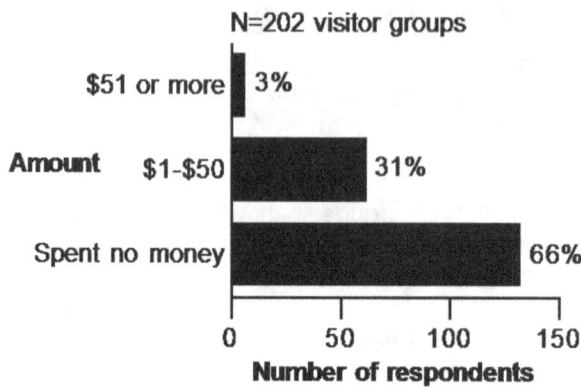

Figure 63. Expenditures for all other purchases inside the park

<u>Donations</u>

- 83% of visitor groups spent no money on donations inside the park (see Figure 64).

- 16% spent $1-$10.

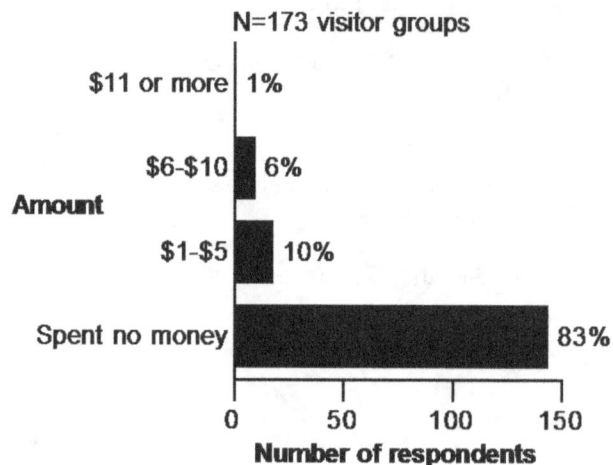

Figure 64. Expenditures for donations inside the park

---

*total percentages do not equal 100 due to rounding
**total percentages do not equal 100 because visitors could select more than one answer

Expenditures in Fort Scott, KS

Question 20b

Please list your group's total expenditures in the city of Fort Scott, KS.

Results

- 34% of visitor groups spent $1-$50 in Fort Scott, KS (see Figure 65).

- 34% spent no money.

- 32% spent $51 or more.

- The average visitor group expenditure in Fort Scott, KS was $74.

- The median group expenditure (50% groups spent more and 50% of groups spent less) was $20.

- The average total expenditure per person (per capita) was $45.

- As shown in Figure 66, the largest proportions of total expenditures in Fort Scott, KS were:

  27% Lodges, hotels, motels, cabins, B&Bs, etc.
  27% Restaurants and bars
  21% Gas & oil

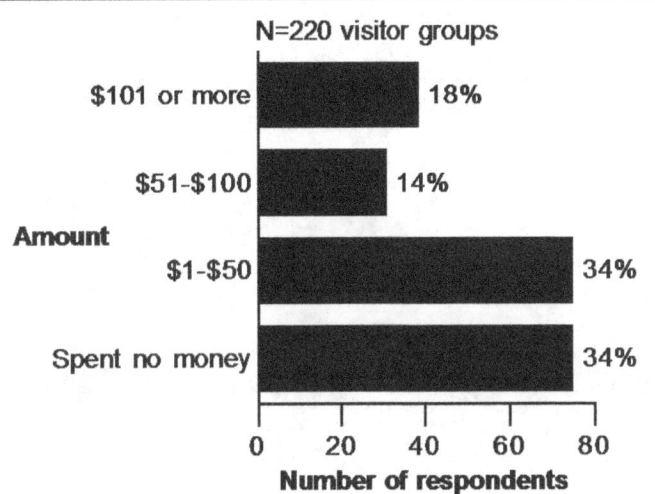

Figure 65. Total expenditures in Fort Scott, KS

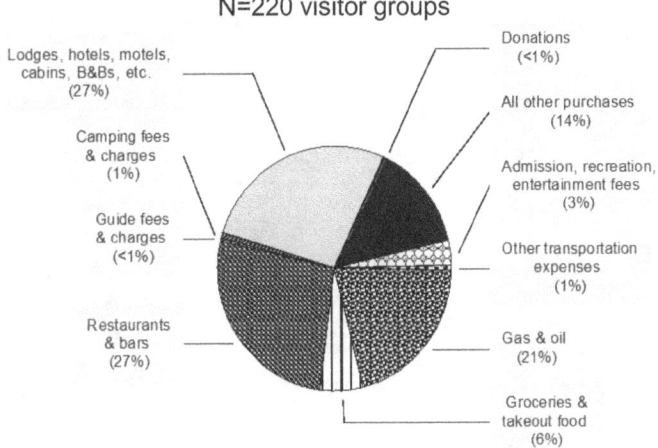

Figure 66. Proportions of total expenditures in Fort Scott, KS

---

*total percentages do not equal 100 due to rounding
**total percentages do not equal 100 because visitors could select more than one answer

Lodges, hotels, motels, cabins, B&Bs, etc.

- 79% of visitor groups spent no money on lodging in Fort Scott, KS (see Figure 67).

- 11% spent $1-$100.

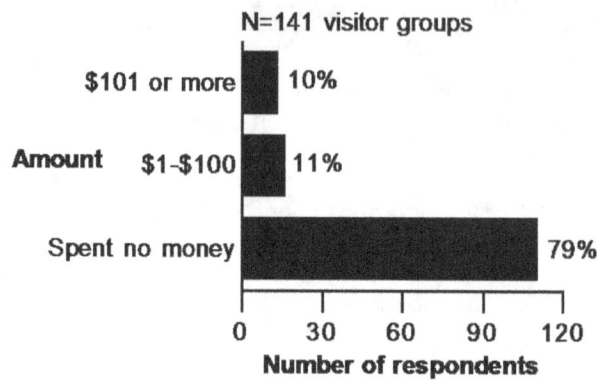

Figure 67. Expenditures for lodging in Fort Scott, KS

Camping fees and charges

- 94% of visitor groups spent no money on camping fees and charges in Fort Scott, KS (see Figure 68).

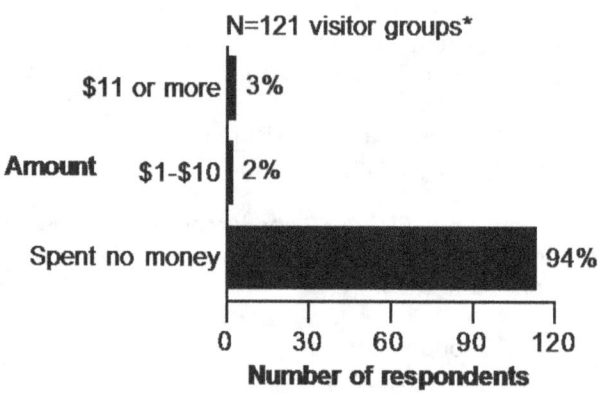

Figure 68. Expenditures for camping fees and charges in Fort Scott, KS

---

*total percentages do not equal 100 due to rounding
**total percentages do not equal 100 because visitors could select more than one answer

Guide fees and charges

- 97% of visitor groups spent no money on guide fees and charges in Fort Scott, KS (see Figure 69).

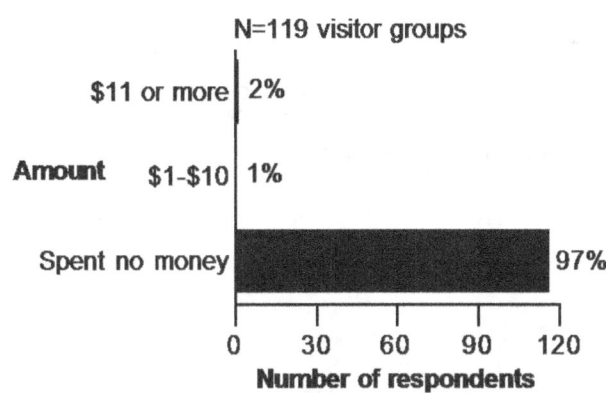

Figure 69. Expenditures for guide fees and charges in Fort Scott, KS

Restaurants and bars

- 46% of visitor groups spent no money on restaurants and bars in Fort Scott, KS (see Figure 70).

- 45% spent $1-$50.

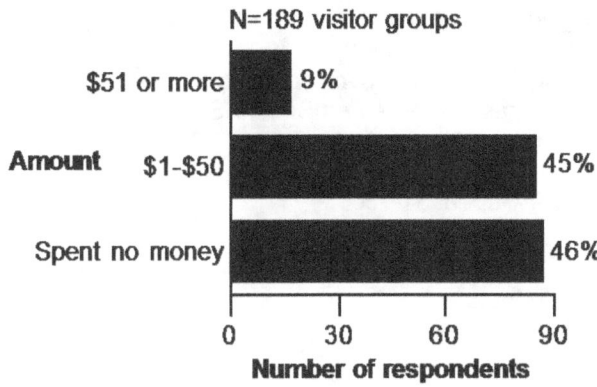

Figure 70. Expenditures for restaurants and bars in Fort Scott, KS

*total percentages do not equal 100 due to rounding
**total percentages do not equal 100 because visitors could select more than one answer

Groceries and takeout food

- 81% of visitor groups spent no money on groceries and takeout food in Fort Scott, KS (see Figure 71).

- 13% spent $11 or more.

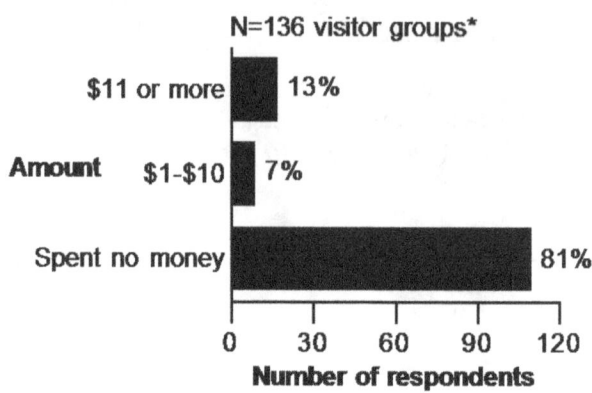

Figure 71. Expenditures for groceries and takeout food in Fort Scott, KS

Gas and oil (auto, RV, boat, etc.)

- 58% of visitor groups spent no money on gas and oil in Fort Scott, KS (see Figure 72).

- 29% spent $1-$50.

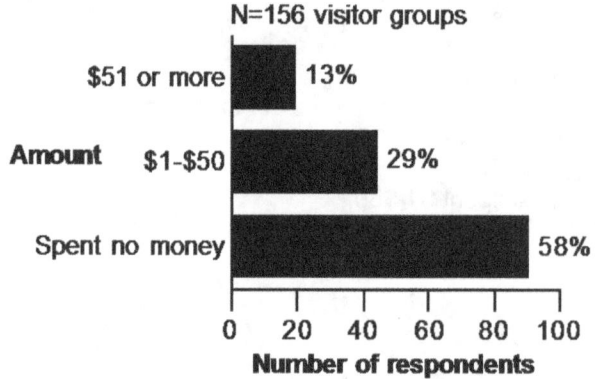

Figure 72. Expenditures for gas and oil in Fort Scott, KS

---

*total percentages do not equal 100 due to rounding
**total percentages do not equal 100 because visitors could select more than one answer

Other transportation (rental cars, taxis, auto repairs, but NOT airfare)

- 99% of visitor groups spent no money on other transportation in Fort Scott, KS (see Figure 73).

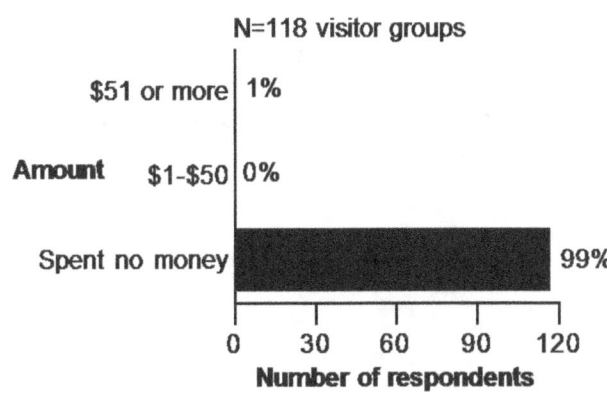

Figure 73. Expenditures for other transportation in Fort Scott, KS

Admission, recreation, and entertainment fees

- 93% of visitor groups spent no money on admission, recreation and entertainment fees in Fort Scott, KS (see Figure 74).

- 6% spent $1-$50.

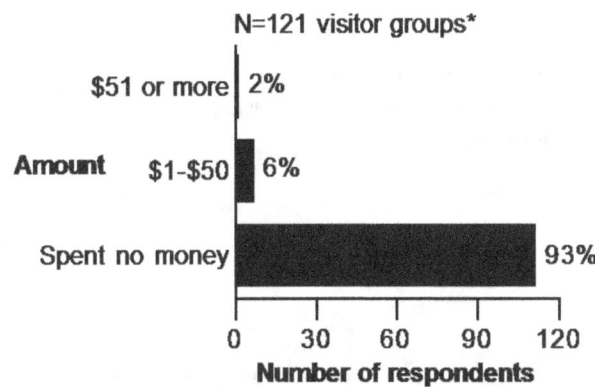

Figure 74. Expenditures for admission, recreation and entertainment fees in Fort Scott, KS

*total percentages do not equal 100 due to rounding
**total percentages do not equal 100 because visitors could select more than one answer

<u>All other purchases</u> (souvenirs, film, books, sporting goods, clothing, etc.)

- 66% of visitor groups spent no money on all other purchases in Fort Scott, KS (see Figure 75).

- 24% spent $1-$50.

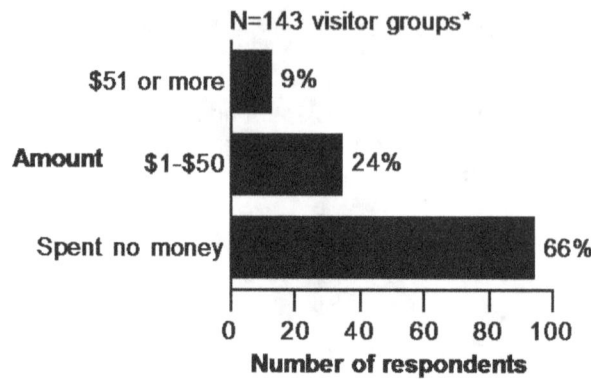

Figure 75. Expenditures for all other purchases in Fort Scott, KS

<u>Donations</u>

- 94% of visitor groups spent no money on donations in Fort Scott, KS (see Figure 76).

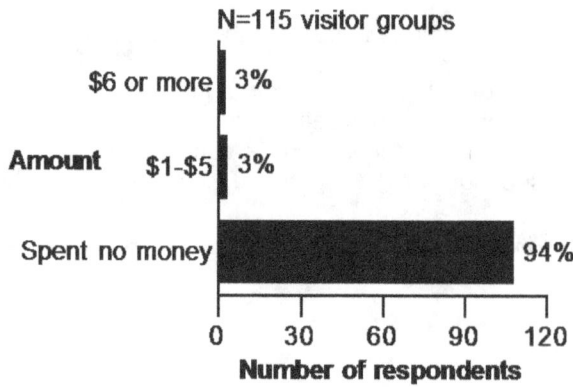

Figure 76. Expenditures for donations in Fort Scott, KS

*total percentages do not equal 100 due to rounding
**total percentages do not equal 100 because visitors could select more than one answer

Preferences for Future Visits

Future visits to the park

Question 21

Would you and your personal group be likely to visit Fort Scott NHS again in the future?

Results

- 67% of visitor groups would likely visit the park in the future (see Figure 77).

- 21% were not sure.

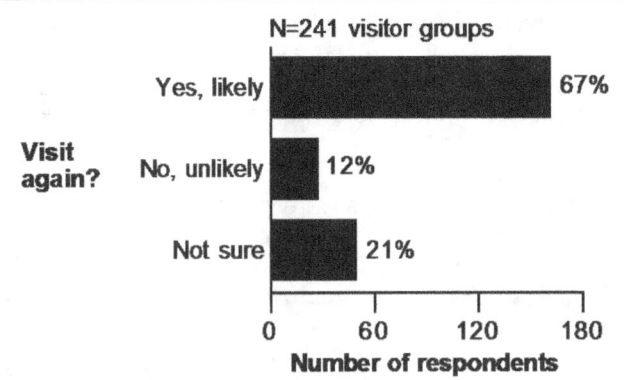

Figure 77. Visitor groups that would likely visit the park in the future

---

*total percentages do not equal 100 due to rounding

**total percentages do not equal 100 because visitors could select more than one answer

Methods to learn about the park's cultural and natural history/features on a future visit

Question 18

If you were to visit Fort Scott NHS in the future, how would you and your personal group prefer to learn about cultural and natural history/features of the park?

Results

- 95% of visitor groups were interested in learning about the park's cultural and natural history/features on a future visit (see Figure 78).

- As shown in Figure 79, the most preferred methods to learn about the park were:

  67% Self-guided tour with brochure
  61% Indoor exhibits
  60% Outdoor exhibits

- "Other" preferences for learning (2%) were:

  Junior Ranger program
  Specific map of the entire area
  Varied formats
  Working site

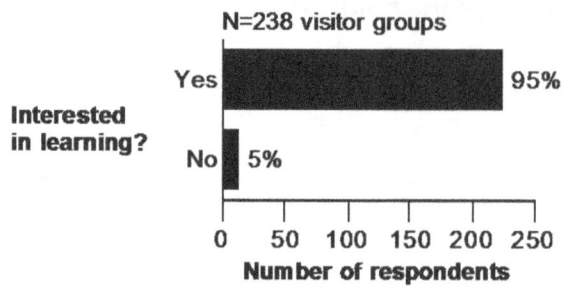

Figure 78. Visitor groups that were interested in learning about the park's cultural and natural history/features on a future visit

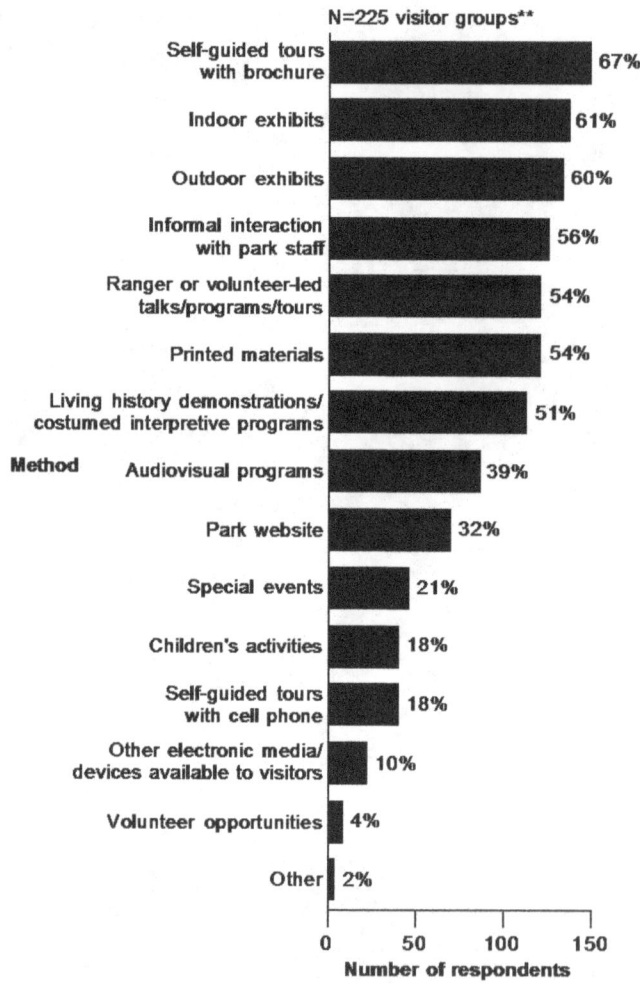

Figure 79. Preferred methods for learning about the park's cultural and natural history/features on a future visit

---

*total percentages do not equal 100 due to rounding

**total percentages do not equal 100 because visitors could select more than one answer

Overall Quality

Question 32
Overall, how would you rate the quality of facilities, services, and recreational opportunities provided to you and your personal group at Fort Scott NHS during this visit?

Results
- 97% of visitor groups rated the overall quality of facilities, services, and recreational opportunities as "very good" or "good" (see Figure 80).

- 1% rated the quality as "very poor."

- No visitor groups rated the quality as "poor."

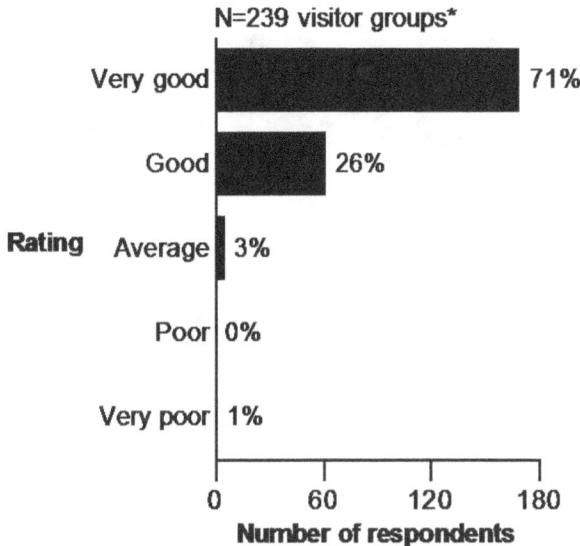

Figure 80. Overall quality rating of facilities, services, and recreational opportunities

---

*total percentages do not equal 100 due to rounding
**total percentages do not equal 100 because visitors could select more than one answer

Visitor Comment Summaries

Planning for the future

Question 30

If you were a manager planning for the future of Fort Scott NHS, what would you and personal group propose? (Open-ended)

Results

- 39% of visitor groups (N=96) responded to this question.

- Table 29 shows a summary of visitor comments.

- The transcribed open-ended comments can be found in the Visitor Comments section.

Table 29. Planning for the future
(N=116 comments; some visitor groups made more than one comment.)

Comment	Number of times mentioned
PERSONNEL (2%)	
Comment	2
INTERPRETIVE SERVICES (47%)	
More living history demonstrations	12
More ranger-led tours	9
More reenactments	5
More historical education/information	4
More interactive activities	4
More children's activities	3
Demonstration exhibit of construction methods	2
Horseback riding	2
More exhibits	2
More ranger-led activities	2
Other comments	10
FACILITIES/MAINTENANCE (8%)	
Park is well-maintained	3
Keep up site maintenance	2
Other comments	4
POLICY/MANAGEMENT (19%)	
Provide access to more areas	5
Advertise park	3
Better signs to the park	2
Other comments	12
RESOURCE MANAGEMENT (1%)	
Comment	1
GENERAL (23%)	
Keep it the way it is	8
Nothing	7
Enjoyed visit	3
Keep up the good work	2
Other comments	7

Additional comments

Question 31a

Is there anything else you and your personal group would like to tell us about your visit to Fort Scott NHS? (Open-ended)

Results

- 45% of visitor groups (N=112) responded to this question.

- Table 30 shows a summary of visitor comments.

- The transcribed open-ended comments can be found in the Visitor Comments section.

Table 30. Additional comments
(N=212 comments; some visitor groups made more than one comment.)

Comment	Number of times mentioned
PERSONNEL (12%)	
Excellent staff	10
Staff is friendly	7
Staff is helpful	7
Other comments	2
INTERPRETIVE SERVICES (25%)	
Very educational	22
Enjoyed exhibits	9
More tours/programs/living history demonstrations	6
Other comments	15
FACILITIES/MAINTENANCE (19%)	
Park is well-maintained	13
Park is clean	9
Excellent facilities	5
Grounds very well-kept	3
Provide drinking fountains/opportunity to purchase water	3
Other comments	7
POLICY/MANAGEMENT (3%)	
Appreciate not having to pay a fee	2
Other comments	5
RESOURCE MANAGEMENT (3%)	
Appreciate restoration and preservation of the site	6
GENERAL (38%)	
Enjoyed visit	28
Well done/keep up the good work	8
Park is interesting	8
Park is nice	8
Thank you	7
It was extremely hot	5
Will return in future	5
We wish we had more time to visit	3
Park is beautiful	2
Other comments	7

Visitor Comments

This section contains transcribed visitor responses to open-ended questions.

Question 30
If you were a manager planning for the future of Fort Scott NHS, what would you and personal group propose? (Open-ended)

- A center court with resting places and interpretive settings
- A guided tour of the site, followed by shopping/lunch in the downtown area
- A living history weekend to celebrate the 150th anniversary of the Civil War
- Access to all areas
- Access to the second floor for disabled
- Activity interactions like Silver Dollar City/George Washington Carver
- Advertise in a much larger area, in more ways, and to keep site maintenance up
- Advertise self better
- Aim to sustain maintenance of facilities
- All looked great to me - very neat, well cared for and informative
- An annual fireworks show provided by Encore Pyrotechnics celebrating birth of fort in April
- Better restroom facilities
- Better signs indicating turn to the site
- Better signs on Highway 50 for traffic coming from west
- Better staff interrelationships with visitors
- Better understanding of what Fort Scott had to offer - plan trip better
- Better viewing of the building methods and a better display of how the fort buildings were constructed
- Bring awareness
- Bring more awareness to battle memorials (soldiers under FS)
- Cannot think of anything you could improve upon
- Continue to fund support to keep exhibits open and up to date
- Cooling stations. That was the hardest part of the trip - the heat.
- Couldn't think of any improvement
- Demonstration (exhibit) of construction methods
- Expanded ranger-led tours and programs
- Expose U.S. history to visitors. Explain the prairie land vs. today's vegetation.
- Flowers planted would add a lot
- For a non-history buff the video narration was a bit boring
- Go in the cool weather
- Greater integration of historic/regional programming in the Fort Scott area across all local attractions/sites. Make Fort Scott a destination with several attractions.
- Guided tour
- Have some people in dress and reenactments
- Historical education
- Historical information
- Horseback riding and/or stable tours
- I think it's fine just the way it is
- I would propose to keep it running the way it is

- o   I'd like to see some of the downtown be made part of the park
- o   If possible, have two guided tours each day instead of one
- o   It was fine in its present condition
- o   Keep entire site as close to original as possible
- o   Keep it open and accessible
- o   Keep it the same
- o   Keep it the way it is!
- o   Keep it the way it is. It is one of the nicest park facilities we have visited.
- o   Keep the SCA guide. Useful and informative.
- o   Keep up the good work
- o   Keep up the good work
- o   Living history demonstrations
- o   Living history events
- o   Make areas such as stables more accessible for visitors to go further in at view
- o   Maps of site, all buildings and purpose of buildings, open more buildings and furnish
- o   Maybe a few more demonstrations
- o   More "living history" events
- o   More costumed volunteers to interact with
- o   More exhibits. Hands-on learning.
- o   More facts and history in brochure, plaques
- o   More historical reenactments or living history programs
- o   More interactive opportunities for kids. Perhaps horses and training like soldiers experienced.
- o   More interpreters in the buildings such as a guard in the jail as an officer in the barracks
- o   More people in costume telling about the different buildings, like the young lady at the hospital, around the site
- o   More ranger-led activities
- o   More ranger-led tours
- o   More reenactments
- o   More than just one reenactment per year
- o   More things to do like puzzles or things to do with your hands
- o   More tours by rangers, children's activities
- o   More videos
- o   My kids love the computer screens that ask questions and help them learn details about the site. I have seen these at other parks.
- o   None
- o   Not having to pay was a big reason we could visit the fort. My grandchildren were able to see the fort.
- o   Not sure
- o   Nothing
- o   Nothing - it was great
- o   Nothing additional
- o   Nothing, because second floor access be very expensive. We were happy with what we were able to access.
- o   Nothing, I love it like it is
- o   Nothing, we enjoyed it all

o   Once a month a working installation
o   Overall, Congress needs to provide the funds to the National Park Service to maintain our parks and sites and to advertise how great they are to the American public
o   Overnight stay as historically accurate as possible
o   Perhaps some reenactments
o   Publicize more on Topeka/Kansas City televisions or Cox Network. Candlelight Christmas tours on different weekends, not just the first weekend of December Rendezvous or living history weekends really publicized. Need to know six months to one year in ad
o   Ranger-led tours
o   Reenactors interpreting history
o   Scavenger hunt type of event
o   Select a fall or spring visit
o   Since site is restored I would schedule more events with groups, i.e. meetings, catered event, etc.
o   Some of the interior displays need more lighting
o   Stay open longer hours
o   To be able to shop for books (especially) and other items in gift shop online
o   Water sold at store
o   We attended Sunday morning - very quiet, nice. Next time at a later time. Busier for talks.
o   We liked the gift shop and touring all the buildings and taking pictures and videos of the displays
o   We would like to be around when you have special events - dressing in period costume, etc.
o   Would love to see more live demonstrations and "acting out" various events of daily life at fort. It would be great if this could occur daily.

Question 31a
Is there anything else you and your personal group would like to tell us about your visit to Fort Scott NHS? (Open-ended)

o   A bit confusing - the numbers in the buildings and map
o   A very pleasant visit
o   All in all well done, well kept up, interesting, helpful in understanding the early western frontier
o   Could be a little more functional
o   Details about bleeding Kansas and interaction with Missouri at the time.
o   Did not spend enough time to do the questionnaire justice
o   Disappointment in staff interaction with visitors. They tend to disappear (the staff not the visitors)
o   Due to temperature of 106 degrees did not revisit as planned due to the heat
o   Easy to access from US 69 and 54 highways
o   Enjoy seeing the constant improvements to the park over the years
o   Enjoyed
o   Enjoyed the site very much
o   Enjoyed, learned. Thank you.
o   Everyone was extremely friendly and very helpful
o   Everyone was friendly, however I would have liked a more "history alive" type of adventure for my kids to garner more appreciation of the event
o   Everyone was so helpful. It was a great visit.
o   Excellent friendly rangers. Everything was clean, nice.
o   Excellent overall job by the National Park Service
o   Fascinating site
o   Fix sidewalks and adjoining dirt/grass to be smooth. Fell during walk from bookstore to other exhibits.
o   Great park, always friendly, helpful staff and clean facilities
o   Had a good time learning about the history of Fort Scott
o   Had potential but nothing scheduled to keep us there very long
o   I am a history buff so I extremely enjoyed Fort Scott and its history. Everything we visit Fort Scott we have learned more.
o   I liked what I had time to see. I wish I had more time. I want to return.
o   I really appreciated the air conditioning in certain places especially when watching the video
o   I thought the site was in very good repair
o   I was not aware of Fort Scott's historic downtown nor its proximity to this park. This may have changed my plans. Certainly worth preserving for future generations. Park staff did an excellent job representing our National Park Service. They are a credit to the site.
o   Impressed with exhibits and buildings. Staff were very helpful. Grounds very well kept.
o   It is a beautiful site - great condition, well done
o   It is a great site - so educational. Kansas' history needs to be documented.
o   It was a very interesting and educational experience
o   It was a very nice and informative visit. My 9 year old daughter wanted to visit.
o   It was during a very hot spell. We could not stay outside for long periods.
o   It was fun
o   It was fun, thank you
o   It was just so hot. Possibly another water fountain outside, or a sidewalk mister. We would have bought cold drinks, if we had seen them.

- It was quite unexpected, but a wonderful experience
- It was very good
- It was very interesting to see the actual housing of that time period of our soldiers and their families
- It was very nice and interesting
- It was very well done. It was a nice stop on our trip.
- It was well maintained. Nice and clean. Liked the sidewalks; they made it easy to walk around the site.
- Keep up the great job
- Learned lots of great information/history through the ranger, who was very excited about his job
- Lots of interesting information from Charlie Meade - Special Deputy US Marshall. Great facilities, great staff.
- Loved the fort - awesome
- More attention to Junior Ranger program. Oath should be administered. Activity book should be reviewed.
- My brother and sister-in-law had been by Fort Scott and invited me to go back with them to see Fort Scott
- My children learned a great deal that they may not have been exposed to if we had not stopped
- My family and I love learning about history. We learned a lot and had a great time. Thank you.
- My grandsons were visiting as from Leander, TX. We picked up their cousins in Devon and came to town for lunch I remembered reading in the Fort Scott paper that the fort was not charging a fee and it gave me the opportunity to take all four to view some
- Perhaps more benches for resting along the tour. Elevators for upper levels would be helpful for those with limitations. Thank you.
- Pleased to find out there is no longer a fee! Finally our taxes at work!
- Probably the best presentation of 19th century life in the USA I have seen
- Quite a few signs had misinformation/misspelled words
- Really enjoyed the video and upstairs rooms
- Scheduled, well-promoted reenactments
- Skip was excellent ranger/historian
- Still could use a fireworks show/annual event to draw in more people and donations
- Thank you for preserving our national treasures and history
- The lady at the greeting desk is an asset to the park. She gave a great introduction. Old construction methods display was excellent.
- The park ranger in the visitor center was wonderful, made the day for our two grandsons.
- The park rangers were very friendly and helpful. We would like a video to buy about Fort Scott.
- The site is beautiful and very clean
- The visit was very enjoyable, informative and it was great to see maintenance being done while we were there
- This is a nice site. We all had a great time.
- Very clean. Lawn had been recently cut. Grass left on sidewalks suggest walks be blown off. Thanks.
- Very enjoyable, staff delightful
- Very friendly staff
- Very good. Had a good guide - Reed Hartford, volunteer.
- Very impressed with facility. Well-cared for/preserved.
- Very informative. Thankful this area is preserved and restored.

- Very interesting
- Very interesting and lovely restoration of site and buildings
- Very interesting, educational, well maintained
- Very interesting. Love American history.
- Very nice
- Very nice park - learned a lot. Rangers helpful.
- Very well maintained and clean, impressive condition
- Very well maintained park.
- Very well put together
- Way too many questions
- We all loved it
- We appreciate and value the National Park Service's and its employees' efforts to preserve Fort Scott
- We enjoy sites like this. Site is extremely well maintained and exhibits have lots of detail that appreciated. Really enjoyed the cell phone tour and displays regarding daily life.
- We enjoyed exploring. It reminded us that we want to be national park rangers/tour guides some day.
- We enjoyed it very much. However, it was extremely hot (over 100 degrees) and there was no water available unless we brought our own into the park.
- We enjoyed our visit. We will come again when our 3-year-old son is older.
- We enjoyed the break from traveling and gaining historical information about our country. I was amazed at the quality of maintenance of the overall facility. It was very clean and inviting.
- We greatly enjoyed visiting the buildings and the piped music around town
- We had a great time
- We had a great visit. All the park rangers did a good job. Keep up the good work.
- We had never seen the site and were just curious.
- We hope to visit again and spend more time in the park and town
- We just hope all sites such as this continue to remain open
- We learned quite a bit. Thank you.
- We think every display was terrific. Supported by artwork and clear, concise information that told us a lot about Fort Scott's purpose and place in history. The place is kept in exceptionally good condition. Thank you very much. In general, each range
- We think it has been very well taken care of. We think that is very important.
- We thoroughly enjoyed our visit
- We thought the ground and buildings were very well kept up and clean and neat as were the grounds - grass mowed and very nice. Would like to stop back by when we had enough time to really see everything.
- We wish we had more time to take a ranger tour
- Well maintained. Informative signage. Interesting interiors.
- Well organized site with friendly and helpful staff. Lots of interesting books.
- Well-maintained and informative
- Wish we had more time to see it, but we do live quite far and not likely to visit the Midwest again for a while
- Wonderful afternoon. Very educational and enjoyable.
- Would have taken guided tour but came in the morning and was done an hour and a half before the tour was to start at 1:00
- Would like to see volunteers in period costume in building exhibits. Museum needs more period artifacts.

- o   Would love to revisit when cooler
- o   Would've been better if not so hot
- o   Youth oriented activities with hands on crafts all the time. School programs to create interest - may already do this. Bus tours.

Appendix 1: The Questionnaire

Appendix 2: Additional Analysis

The Visitor Services Project (VSP) offers the opportunity to learn from VSP visitor study data through additional analysis. Two-way and three-way cross tabulations can be made with any questions.

Below are some examples of the types of cross tabulations that can be requested. To make a request, please use the contact information below, and include your name, address and phone number in the request.

1. What proportion of family groups with children attends interpretive programs?

2. Is there a correlation between visitors' ages and their preferred sources of information about the park?

3. Are highly satisfied visitors more likely to return for a future visit?

4. How many international visitors participate in hiking?

5. What ages of visitors would use the park website as a source of information on a future visit?

6. Is there a correlation between visitor groups' rating of the overall quality of their park experience and their ratings of individual services and facilities?

7. Do larger visitor groups (e.g., four or more) participate in different activities than smaller groups?

8. Do frequent visitors rate the overall quality of their park experiences differently than less frequent visitors?

The VSP database website (http://vsp.uidaho.edu) allows data searches for comparisons of data from one or more parks.

For more information please contact:

Visitor Services Project, PSU
College of Natural Resources
P.O. Box 441139
University of Idaho
Moscow, ID 83843-1139

Phone: 208-885-7863
Fax: 208-885-4261
Email: littlej@uidaho.edu
Website: http://www.psu.uidaho.edu

Appendix 3: Decision Rules for Checking Non-response Bias

There are several methods for checking non-response bias. However, the most common way is to use some demographic indicators to compare between respondents and non-respondents (Dey 1997; Salant and Dillman 1994; Dillman and Carley-Baxter 2000; Dillman, 2007; Stoop 2004). In this study, group type, group size, age of the group member (at least 16 years old) completing the survey, whether the park was the primary reason for being in the area, and respondent's place of residence were five variables that were used to check for non-response bias.

Two independent-sample T-tests were used to test the differences between respondents and non-respondents. The p-values represent the significance levels of these tests. If the p-value is greater than 0.05, the two groups are judged to be insignificantly different.

Chi-square tests were used to detect the difference in the group types, whether the park is the primary reason for being in the area, and respondent's place of residence. The hypotheses were there would be no significant difference between respondents and non-respondents in terms of who they travelled with, why they were in the area, or where they came from. If the p-value is greater than 0.05, the differences are judged to be insignificant.

The hypotheses for checking non-response bias are: Respondents and non-respondents are not significantly difference in term of

1. Average age
2. Number of people they were travelling with in a personal group
3. Type of group which they were travelling with
4. Primary reason for travelling to the area
5. Proximity from home to the park

As shown in Tables 2-5, respondents and non-respondents were not significantly different in terms of group size, group type, primary reason for travelling to the area, and proximity from home to the park. The p-value for respondent/non-respondent average age is less than 0.05, indicating significant difference between respondents and non-respondents. In regard to age difference, various reviews of survey methodology (Dillman and Carley-Baxter 2000; Goudy 1976, Filion 1976, Mayer and Pratt Jr. 1967) have consistently found, that in public opinion surveys, average respondent ages tend to be higher than average non-respondent ages. This difference is often caused by other reasons such as availability of free time rather than problems with survey methodology. In addition, because unit of analysis for this study is a visitor group, the group member who received the questionnaire may be different than the one who actually completed it after the visit. Sometimes the age of the actual respondent is higher than the age of the group member who accepted the questionnaire at the park. The results indicated younger respondents may be underrepresented in the results but overall non-response bias is judged to be insignificant.

References

Dey, E. L. (1997). Working with Low Survey Response Rates: The Efficacy of Weighting Adjustment. *Research in Higher Education*, 38(2): 215-227.

Dillman, D. A. (2007). *Mail and Internet Surveys: The Tailored Design Method, Updated version with New Internet, Visual, and Mixed-Mode Guide*, 2nd Edition, New York: John Wiley and Sons, Inc.

Dillman, D. A. and Carley-Baxter, L. R. (2000). *Structural determinants of survey response rate over a 12-year period, 1988-1999*, Proceedings of the section on survey research methods, 394-399, American Statistical Association, Washington, D.C.

Filion, F. L. (Winter 1975-Winter 1976). Estimating Bias due to Non-response in Mail Surveys. *Public Opinion Quarterly*, Vol 39 (4): 482-492.

Goudy, W. J. (1976). Non-response Effect on Relationships Between Variables. *Public Opinion Quarterly*. Vol 40 (3): 360-369.

Mayer, C. S. and Pratt Jr. R. W. (Winter 1966-Winter 1967). A Note on Non-response in a Mail Survey. *Public Opinion Quarterly*. Vol 30 (4): 637-646.

Salant, P. and Dillman, D. A. (1994). *How to Conduct Your Own Survey*. U.S.: John Wiley and Sons, Inc.

Stoop, I. A. L. (2004). Surveying Non-respondents. *Field Methods*, 16 (1): 23.

NPS 471/115207, June 2012